/\

COUGAR KILLER

By Jay C. Bruce, Sr.

High-Lonesome Books
Silver City, New Mexico

ISBN-13: 978-0-944383-73-5
ISBN-10: 0-9447383-73-4

First published by Comet Press Books, NY, 1953

This printing, 2007
by
High-Lonesome Books
P.O. Box 878
Silver City, New Mexico 88062

DEDICATION

In consideration of the value of our wildlife resources to both the spiritual and physical well-being of mankind, I dedicate this work to the promotion of an effective program to increase all species of game birds and animals found in every section of these United States of America.

CONTENTS

I

COLLECTING COUGARS FOR THE
UNIVERSITY OF CALIFORNIA

/\

Outlaws — Animal and Human

THINKING back over the thirty years I spent hunting mountain lions for the California Fish and Game Commission, I find that 1924 is impressed in my memory as being the one most particularly fraught with experiences involving interest and dangers, as well as incidents revealing the family life of *Felis concolor californica* — commonly known as mountain lion, panther or cougar.

In the beginning of that year I made a memorable hunting trip to a famous area — that adjoining the western boundary of General Grant National Park, in Fresno County. Long famed for its forests of giant redwood trees *(Sequoia gigantea),* it later became the gateway to the newly acquired Kings Canyon National Park, which rivals Yosemite in scenic wonders.

In addition to the possibility of its providing a good catch of the big cats, this area had a special appeal to me because of its colorful history, it having been the refuge used by the outlaws Chris Evans and the Sontag brothers, George and John, accused of train robberies during the early 1890's. I still remembered having heard my parents read the accounts of those escapades, written by Joaquin Miller, who was sent there by a San Francisco newspaper to report the details of the prolonged manhunt. One pertinent sentence from the colorful pen of the prominent writer and naturalist still stuck in my memory. It was: "The way the wind blows in these parts, all those living along the road between Visalia and

Sequoia Mills say they would rather have Chris Evans in their homes than any of those who are hunting him." This sentiment, impressed in the minds and hearts of people who had known Evans for years, probably accounts for the outlaws having been able to avoid capture for several years, while making periodic visits to the Evans family home in Visalia, county seat of Tulare County.

When the outlaws were finally taken, it was rumored that they had been betrayed by one of their own gang, who wanted to give up. In any event, John Sontag was missing from the scene of capture at Stone Corral, on the road between Visalia and Badger in Tulare County. George Sontag was killed, while Chris Evans was wounded by bullets which smashed his left arm and gouged out his left eye. Even then he managed to take to the brush and walk several miles and hide in a rancher's hay loft, where he was discovered and turned over to the sheriff by the rancher. When the news reached Wawona, where our homestead was situated, the big talk was about Hiram Rappelje, who had led the posse that made the killing. You see, Hi Rappelje was well known to all of us, since he had been employed to drive a "coach and four" on the Yosemite Stage and Turnpike Company line, owned by Albert Henry Washburn and John Jay Cook — both uncles to me by marriage.

The opportunity for me to visit this area for the first time came early in January, 1924, when our game warden, Art Bullard, living at Dunlap, wrote to our home office, reporting that lion sign was plentiful on McKenzie Ridge and around Millwood, and that deer were being exterminated by the big cats. Joe Hunter, in charge of our office, approved of an immediate lion hunt in that section.

Knowing that the Museum of Vertebrate Zoology of the University of California was anxious to have specimens from all parts of the state, I thought it would be worthwhile for the Museum to send a zoologist along with me to record data and to care for specimens (hides and skeletons). Therefore I telephoned Dr. Joseph Grinnel, director of that institution, explaining the possibilities. Dr. Grinnel assigned Joe Dixon, one of their most experienced naturalists, for the task. Dixon had previously accompanied me on three lion hunts since June 1920, during which time we became very good friends.

Leaving my home near Haywards, Alameda County, early on a stormy, January morning, we drove an old Dodge the 200 miles to Dunlap, arriving there around six o'clock that evening, after churning through mud hub-deep for forty miles from Fresno on. Since Art had no room for us, we put up for the night at the Greeley Ranger Station five miles farther on. Ray Stephens, the district ranger, who had hunted with me three years before in Tuolumne County, made us all comfortable, including my four lion dogs, Eli, Ranger, Scout and Duke, who were billeted in the barn. That evening I talked to Bullard over the Forest Service telephone and arranged to use a two-room cabin (known as the Green house) belonging to his brother-in-law. Situated in the lion country on McKenzie Ridge at an elevation of 5000 feet, it seemed suitable for a permanent base camp. The game warden offered to guide us to it and spend a few days with us, until we became acquainted with the lay of the land.

During the night the rain changed to snow, covering the ground with a layer four inches thick by daybreak. Climbing some 3000 feet in 10 miles, we found the snow increasing in depth as we proceeded, until it was some 12 inches deep in the vicinity of the Green house when we reached there, about noon. Just as we caught the first view of our new camp, something still more interesting caught my eye — a line of round depressions four inches across and spaced some twenty inches apart in the snow, which revealed that a lion had crossed the road some time during the previous night — probably about midnight, when the snow was about eight inches thick on the ground. Four inches more had fallen and half filled the impression since the hunting feline had passed here.

Ordinarily, I would have started the dogs on the trail at once, but this afternoon there was more immediate work to be done to make the camp more comfortable for men and dogs. Wood had to be gathered and chopped into stove lengths; bedding places had to be provided for the dogs, under the cabin-floor, which was some two and a half feet above the ground on the downhill or front side of the building. The kitchen part contained a stove of family size and in fair shape. A rough board table and several rickety chairs made up the other furniture.

The storm ended by 8 P.M., leaving conditions perfect for lion trailing the next day. However, we failed to find any more lion signs during the next two days of hunting. Finally I decided to move camp to Samson Flat, some fifteen hundred feet lower and on the northern or Kings River side of the divide, where Art Bullard's brother, Will, had a log-cabin cow-camp. Will had been seeing lion tracks around there at regular intervals during the last summer, Art said.

To transport supplies to Will's place it was necessary to pack them on horses, or drag them for two miles down a steep sled-road. Will packed the horse while Art, Joe and I hunted ahead with the dogs. After waiting a half an hour at the camp, we decided to make a scouting trip westward toward the Delilah lookout station. Within ten minutes, and a half a mile, we struck fresh tracks of a female lion who had come down the trail we were going up, and turned to her left — southward. The dogs took off on the run on a course which crossed the trail we'd traveled some forty minutes earlier. If we had started from our first camp a few minutes later, we would have struck the cat's hot trail some three hundred yards from our new camp and bagged her near there. Or if we had not waited 30 minutes at Will Bullard's cabin, the same thing would have been possible.

As it happened, this half hour of grace gave the feline prowler time to reach the 1500-foot crest of a steep ridge a mile to the east before the dogs came near to catching up to her. By the time we reached the top, twenty minutes later, the dogs were barking "treed" a mile down Dark Canyon farther east. When we reached the tree our quarry was rested and ready to make another run for her life. But both Art and I were ready too and beat her to the jump with two pistol bullets through her chest. In spite of this the cat left her mark on all three dogs before giving up her "nine lives." Dixon wanted the hide and skeleton, while I needed the cat meat for dog food. We took turns at carrying the 90-pound body for a mile or more down canyon to a trail, where Will Bullard could pick it up next day with a horse. A three-mile climb up the trail to camp finished the day's work.

Two days later Art Bullard and I trailed a full-grown male lion upward along a ridge dividing the basins of Sampson Flat and Davis Flat to the northwest. Since the tracks were two days old trailing was slow. Pointing to a rocky knoll ahead, Art, who was a member of the second generation of his family raised in this vicinity, said: "That knoll used to be one of the hide-outs used by the outlaws Chris Evans and the Sontag brothers, George and John, during the early 1890's. It overlooked the country all around before the brush was allowed to grow so high and thick."

Now, we had to crawl and wedge our way under or between the bushes at a snail's pace. When the dogs, several hundred feet ahead of us, came to this knoll, they pepped up in voice and doubled their speed. There was only one explanation and I gave it: "The cat slept there yesterday and now we have a track twelve hours fresher, at the least."

Sure enough, there was his bed in a woodrat's nest scattered between two screening rocks surrounded by rotten remnants of boxes and blankets once used to furnish this former lair of the notorious train robbers. Strangely enough (or would you say appropriately), this wasteful feline killer, member of a tribe outlawed practically all over the United States, had chosen to travel the same course and sleep in the same bed, so to speak, as did his counterparts in the human race a third of a century earlier.

As we trailed along, Art Bullard told me that several mountaineers of those days knew about this hang-out, but wouldn't give it away because they believed that the accused men were being railroaded to prison. Art himself thought they were guilty because the trouble started soon after the railroad detectives threw Chris Evans' family out by force from a house they had built on land granted to the railroad by the U. S. Government. "Anyhow," said Art, "they killed two men when a posse closed in on them at the Jim Young cabin on the mountain above Dunlap." "What happened to the rest of the posse?" I asked. "Two of them were Indian guides, who disappeared after pointing out the cabin," he replied. "As for the others, a half dozen or so, they scattered like quail in the brush and came straggling into Dunlap, one at a time, for a couple of days afterwards."

The dogs were gaining on us and nearly to the crest of Delilah Ridge, so we had to stop talking and save our breath for climbing. By the time we reached the ridge line, the dogs were baying "lost trail"— a long bay followed by a short one — at the snow-line half way down the farther side toward White Deer Valley. "The snow has melted since the lion passed there, and the scent had gone with it," I explained, "so we had just as well call it a day and go back to camp."

Art decided to follow the ridge road for three miles to Samson Flat Saddle where he'd left his pickup and go home to attend to his own work. I began sounding my hunting horn in long-held notes to call the dogs back and save their feet and energy for another day and fresher tracks. Almost immediately the sound of another horn came to us from the vicinity of a cabin we could see at the edge of the valley some fifteen hundred feet below us and half a mile away by the slope. This other horn and mine sounded so nearly alike that the notes from either one might be mistaken for an echo from the other one's blast. In fact, I was confused until the sounds kept coming from below while mine was silent. Then we noticed that the tooter of the other horn sounded one long note, followed by two short ones, repeating them at short intervals.

Suddenly it occurred to me that the dogs might be fooled into thinking I was calling them to a track, and run down to the cabin in the valley. So I did my best to out-toot the other fellow and call the dogs back to us, while we waited some twenty minutes on the ridge. Then Eli came and was soon followed by Ranger and Duke. But Scout failed to appear. Finally we decided to go down, pick up Scout and proceed two miles farther down the valley to Alex Jones' cow-camp and stay there overnight. When halfway down, we heard a new note, a long one. A minute or two later the old signal, a long and two short, was sounded and repeated twice.

As we descended, Art explained that the cabin we saw belonged to a Texan named Moore, who had homesteaded there and was trying to raise hogs on the acorns dropped by white oaks and live oaks which were abundant in the vicinity. Coming near the cabin we saw Scout snooping around in the yard. Now, I was sore, thinking this stranger had tooted his horn to interfere with our hunting. I approached the cabin with fire in my eyes. Out of the door came a withered runt of a man well past middle age, with a cow's horn in one hand while his jaws worked dextrously on a quid of tobacco. "Why in hell did you have to blow that horn and call my dogs down here?" I scolded. His face went red while his thin, graying but partly sandy colored hair fairly stood up like that of a terrier on the fight. With a flourish he brought the horn to his lips and gave out with one long blast followed by two short ones, and repeated the same call twice. Then stepping up to me he yelped: "Who in hell are you to tell me I can't toot my own horn on my own place? I'll toot it just as much as I damn please. To-o-o-t, toot," he blasted. Then turning toward me with an air of defiance he challenged: "I'd like to see the color of any man's hair who can stop me from tooting my horn on my own dung-hill. You're pretty damn big, but I've got a Winchester in here that says you're not big enough." He started for the door and then changed his mind, turned and said, "Hello there, Bullard," as though he had just noticed Art. Art introduced me as the lion hunter, and explained why I was so put out about the affair. With that the Texan flared up again, glanced from under shaggy eyebrows and yelped, rather than asked: "Don't your hounds know the sound of your horn by this time?" "Yours and mine sound much alike," I answered. "They don't neither," he shouted. "Too-oo-oo-oot, toot, toot, now you toot yours and we'll see." I gave one long blast. He looked confused. I followed up with a suggestion: "Let's change horns, I'd like to try yours." We did. "Blow a long and two shorts," he ordered. I did, and he followed suit. You couldn't tell which was which. "Well, maybe you can't blame the hounds, after all," he admitted. "Maybe they got more sense than we have. At least they're not wrangling," I replied.

"Which way you fellers going?" he inquired. Art told him. "Well, it's past noon, so you-all had better come in and have some sow-belly and beans with flap-jacks, and coffee to wash it down," he invited. "That's enough for anybody," I said, "but we ate a cold lunch on the way." "Yes," Art said, "we better be going and see how things are at Alex's cabin."

"Stop in and have a bite whenever either one of you come by; you're always welcome now, since we've got acquainted. So-long." "So-long," we answered.

As soon as we were out of ear-shot, I said: "That old guy acted crazier than a bed bug." "Yes, crazy like a fox," Art snorted. "Didn't you catch on that he was giving signals with that horn? That's all he has it for."

"What kind of signals?"

"Signals to someone out hunting deer, probably his son. Everyone around here knows that you're hunting lions in this neck of the woods. You see I passed out the word when you wrote and asked me to get in touch with all the mountaineers and cattlemen and have them watch for lion tracks and report them to me. Besides, I gave the information to Mrs. McGee, too, and she wrote it up for the Fresno papers. By this time every one knows that I'm helping you get started."

I was beginning to get the drift, but Art went on: "The way I figure it; the old man heard the hounds coming his way and signaled; don't shoot or bring in a deer, — a long note and two short ones. Then when you called the dogs back and things quieted down, he signaled all is clear by giving one long note. That was the one we heard when halfway down the mountain. Then Scout arrived there and the old fellow thought we might be close behind and tooted the warning signal again. He was coming out to toot again when he saw us and, of course, had to keep quiet or risk giving himself away. Before he could think of an excuse to sound off, you gave him just the right opening by bawling him out. Of course he was sore; but not enough to prevent him from sounding the warning. Then you spoiled that by sounding a long note. When you changed horns he made sure you sounded the warning too, by ordering you to toot a long and two shorts. He was bluffing when he pretended he was going for the gun, for the gun wasn't there. His son had it out hunting. He's staying with the old man, but you notice we didn't see him around the place."

Well, Art had something there. It all added up. As a game warden he was tops—a natural born man-hunter. Then why was it he did not lie in wait for the violator and catch him if he brought in a deer? Simply because it was not the sensible thing to do while I was working this area with my valuable, thoroughly trained dogs. We both knew this but did not discuss it.

(Incidentally, a couple of years later the tough Texan sent for me to come to his place and kill a lion which had been praying on his hogs. "He's a big one and comes in here regular every week or so. He's eating me out of house and home. One night he killed three hogs worth fifty dollars in all. I hope you get him, or I'll have to go out of the hog-raising game." He didn't have to quit—I got the lion three days later. There was no doubt that it was the pork lover, for the hog-killing ended with his death. After being told on this occasion that I made it a practice not to meddle in the duties of the game wardens, my host, referring to our first meeting, confirmed every detail of Art Bullard's analysis of that comedy. "I had to warn the boy, and that was the only way I could do it after you fellows got here," he apologized.)

To return to the lion hunt that was interrupted by the

wily old man—After spending the night at Alex Jones' homestead, I started a ten-mile hunt the next morning, going back to Samson Flat via White-Deer Saddle, a depression of the ridge dividing the watersheds of the Kings River and Mill Creek to the south. Meanwhile Alex was to take Art to Dunlap by auto. The route I chose was one which tomcat nature would consider ideal for a beat, one way or another. So I expected to find this one's tracks pointing eastward to complete a circuit, which in this case, must trace a sort of irregular figure eight. So it was in a spirit of anxious expectancy that I reached White-Deer Saddle. Before I could scan the frozen ground, Ranger, fifty feet ahead, gave out a long-held, joyously toned bay. Instantly the other hounds joined in to make a thrilling chorus, while the silent trailer, Eli, took off in the lead, toward Delilah Lookout.

The feline outlaw had played my game so far, and chances of his living out this day were mighty slim. After an hour or so of racing up the general rise of the ridge, the dogs went out of hearing. Evidently they hadn't gone over Delilah Peak and on along the ridge, the natural course for a hunting panther to follow, because they had gone out of my hearing range too suddenly for that. They must have turned off the ridge to the left and downward behind a spur on the northern slope of the Peak. Yet I couldn't imagine any tomcat going that way unless it was to bed for the day in the seclusion of some out of the way jungle or bluff. Still this seemed unlikely because our quarry had apparently come this far before midnight, for tracks made in patches of snow had punctured nearly to the ground and the pad-prints were iced over, thus proving they were made before the snow crusted after the day's thawing.

But maybe the cat had killed a deer near here, fed and bedded close by. This would account for the sudden burst of speed necessary to take the hounds out of hearing while I was less than half a mile behind them. In an attempt to find the trail, I turned to my left, intending to follow a curving course, one which would cut every patch of snow. Soon

I came to a blood-stained patch covered with numerous dark stains made by sixteen mud-soiled canine paws on the run. Big cat tracks, with widespread toe marks pointing backwards toward the trail their maker had left, were sunken full depth in the snow, thus indicating the killer had moved backward while dragging his kill. Following a trail marked by deer hair, intestines and gobs of their vegetable contents for some three hundred feet, I came to a mound composed of pine needles and black-oak leaves piled three feet high against the uphill side of a fallen tree trunk four feet thick. The ground on that side had been raked clean by big cat toes and claws over an area twenty feet or so in diameter. A magnificent set of antlers protruded from under one end of the mound. I scattered the covering and revealed the gutted carcass of a magnificent buck that must have weighed more than two hundred pounds. Cat-like, the killer had devoured the liver and tenderloins first. I coveted those ten-point antlers and thought of taking them along, but a change in the breeze brought to my alert ears the faint sounds of barking and baying, canine music sweet to any lion hunter's ears.

"The game is treed, come and get it," they were announcing and beseeching, wild with excitement and impatience. Testing the breeze, I found it was coming from the northeast; I headed that way on the run, fighting through thickets, scrambling over rocks and fallen trees, sliding down into and climbing up out of gulch after gulch, stopping now and then for a few anxious seconds to listen for the thrilling sounds of dogs barking "treed." Sometimes, as I topped a rise, they seemed to be near, then, at other times, the sounds died out as I dropped into gulches.

At last I climbed onto a northeast spur of Delilah—there they were, baying and barking furiously, no more than three hundred yards ahead of and half that far below me. Loading the 38-40 revolver as I ran, I was ready when I reached the spot and saw the worried panther at bay twenty feet up, between the forks of a small oak tree. Flattened ears and twitching tail-tip told me the cat was getting annoyed at the whole business. He had been up there long enough to get back his wind and was ready to make another race for freedom. This I did not want, since it might end up in the bottom of Kings River Canyon. Two tree forks protected the lion's chest on both sides. I tried to maneuver so as to send a bullet through the front of his husky chest and into his heart.

The dogs must have sensed the cat's intentions for they separated to surround the tree. The panther sprang toward Eli. I fired. The cat crumpled in mid-air and landed half limp with a shattered spine, and rolled downhill biting and clawing at everything within reach of his jaws and forepaws. My bullet had passed through about midway between head and tail. The dog pack closed in. Duke got the first hold on the stricken cat's throat, while the other dogs attacked the rear. I barged into the melee, as the master killer gripped Duke between his two forepaws, armed with ten sharp claws nearly two inches long. The hound held on. The cat flipped him over endwise, thus bringing the dog's thigh into his mouth and spoiling my chance for a head shot. Duke let go as the lion socked four teeth through his thigh muscle. Pushing the revolver muzzle against the lion's scalp, I fired. The cat's jaw clamped tight as his muscles went rigid. Duke howled and tugged. Shoving the gun barrel between the lion's jaws I forced them apart to release Duke. Still game, the hound, with blood streaming from his wounds, wobbled back to attack the quivering body.

Now, I had a pair of specimens, a male and a female from this locality, for Dixon to take to the State University. Leaving the lion corpse where it died, I put a rope on Duke and led him slowly to the nearest trail, helping him over the rough spots. Then releasing him I let him take his time following me to Samson Flat. There I fixed a comfortable bed for him in the saddle-room adjoining one end of the log cabin. Mostly, I let him be his own doctor, making a routine examination morning and evening, for signs of possible infection.

From my description of the gulch where the lion was killed,

Will Bullard was able to locate the carcass easily enough the next day and pack it into camp on his horse. The cat's weight was 140 pounds; its length was nearly 7 feet.

While I had been hunting down the male lion, Joe Dixon had spent his time investigating, measuring and photographing several dens in which bears had been found hibernating several winters before. He also took measurements and photographs of a leaning yellow pine which had provided a sheltered bed for the male lion sometime previous to our arrival here. The base of this tree had been hollowed out by fire so that a cavity 4 feet long, 3 feet wide, and 1 foot deep had been formed on the southern side of the tree which leaned in that direction, thus providing a suitable shelter from storm. When I discovered it on a previous hunt I deduced that the lion had killed a deer within a few hundred feet and bedded here between meals. My deduction was based on two large piles of dung near the tree, indicating its occupant had digested two full meals during his occupancy of this temporary lair.

Let me interrupt my story for a bit here to give some pointers on the science of lion hunting.

Any mountaineer or academic naturalist might well have thought that our work here was finished, since tracks of this pair of panthers were all we had seen so far. But years of studying panther nature first-hand had taught me that there should be a family of young lions (possibly as many as four) within four or five miles of Samson Flat. They might be of any age and size between three months old (15 pounds in weight for the female, 20 pounds for the male) and a year old (70 pounds for a female and 88 pounds for a male). At the latter age young lions are left to shift for themselves, since the mother comes in season again and deserts them to seek a mate.

The fact that the female we had taken was traveling after sunrise, and taking the shortest route from west to east, indicated that she had been hunting toward the west all night, killed a deer, and was hurrying back, as directly as

was practicable, to get to her young, which had been left at
a former kill east of our camp. That her offspring were older
than the weaning age—two months—by at least a month was
revealed by lack of any signs of milk in the six breasts of the
dead lioness. On the other hand, they couldn't be more than
a year old. If they happened to be, say 13 months old, their
dam would have already come in season, abandoned them,
joined the male and been found traveling with him for ten
days or so. After that she would have gone her own way,
hunting by night when she needed to, and sleeping by day,
instead of cat-walking hastily past a human habitation in
broad daylight, with her stomach full of freshly killed venison. If she had even recently satisfied the mating urge, then
evidence of pregnancy would have been noticeable in her
reproduction organs. Since this was not the case, our next
move should be to go hunting to the east—the direction this
mother cat was heading when the dogs overtook her.

A couple of days after bagging the male lion, I took off
on the exact course the female had taken up to the crest of
the ridge to the east the morning we bagged her. Duke had
to be left in camp to recover from his injuries. Will Bullard
would feed and care for him in case I failed to return that
evening. Old tracks of both cat and dogs were still visible
in spots of soft earth among the rocks. These showed that the
lioness had turned up-ridge after reaching the crest-line,
and proceeded along it for some three hundred yards before
sensing that the baying hounds were dogging her footsteps.
Then she became alarmed for the safety of her young ones
and herself and turned off to the left, running down Dark
Canyon to lead the dog-pack away from the place where
her offspring were located.

A half-mile farther up ridge I found lion tracks of two
sizes. The smaller ones were not quite large enough to have
been made by the paws of an adult female—they were some
three-eighths of an inch smaller each way. I estimated they
were made by the paws of a female eleven months old and
65 pounds in weight. The larger one were too large to have

been made by an adult female but too small to fit the paws of an adult male—about halfway between the two in width and length. They must have been made by the paws of a male of the same age as the female. This combination of signs indicated the two cats were litter brother and sister.

Since the lions had prowled here two days ago, the scent was faint for a quarter-mile, until we entered the upper end of Blue Canyon. Here the ground had been criss-crossed by a maze of cat tracks over an area of five or six hundred feet each way. The hide and cleanly picked skeleton of a large doe near the center of the area tracked over proved the pair had spent several days and nights hanging around here, while waiting for their mother to return.

From here on the scent was fresher by some twenty hours, I judged, since the dogs progressed twice as fast. After five hours of difficult trailing along as many miles of a meandering course which took us into canyon after canyon where snow was two feet deep in many places on the northern slope of McKenzie Ridge, we came to a southern turn of the topography of the watershed which drained into Mill-Flat Creek. On this eastern facing slope the morning sun had melted away the thin covering of snow. Since our double quarry had passed along here early the night before, all scent and visible signs of tracks had gone with the snow.

We were eight miles from Samson Flat by the route we had come and some three miles farther by road. My forest service map showed a branch road on the far side of Mill-Flat Creek. Looking across to try to locate it, I detected some kind of animals—two of them, moving slowly up the road three hundred yards away as the crow flies. Finally I made them out to be a man riding a donkey and leading another one. I hadn't heard of anyone who was supposed to be in that out of the way locality. What business could anyone have there, unless it was to hide out and stretch their grub supply by killing deer for meat?

Maybe the man was occupying one of two ramshackle cabins near Millwood a mile upstream. Art had told me about these cabins, stating that the fire guard for the forest service used them during the summer. One was furnished with a small stove, a table, shelves, a few kettles, a coffee-pot and dishes enough, of a sort, to accommodate two people. The other one was used to store hay and grain needed for the guard's saddle-horse. I thought I had better follow up the stranger and find out if he was camping there, because I intended to move in myself, so as to be nearer the place where the lion tracks were lost. Besides, this road led to one·which provided the easiest route of travel to the Green house and on to Samson Flat.

Within five minutes I reached the road, and was surprised to learn by the tracks in the mud that three men had gone down the road and that two came up it a couple of days before. Where the road crossed a shady gulch a half-mile farther up toward Millwood I came upon a model-T-Ford stalled in drifted snow two feet deep. Grouped around it were two husky young men, an under-sized older one, two young women, and two skinny donkeys saddled with pack outfits. All of them except the donkeys appeared to be confused at my appearance. Glancing in the tonneau I saw two full bags marked ground corn and one marked sugar. "What in the world are you going to do with all that corn and sugar?" I asked. "Feed it to the jackasses, what we don't eat ourselves," replied the runt. "Where are you staying?" I asked. "In those two old cabins still standing where the old Good sawmill use to be, about four miles down the creek," the runt explained. "What in the world do you folks find to do there?" I inquired. "We have a gold mine farther down the creek and are going to work it this winter," he explained. "Is it any good?" I asked. "It pays all right," he answered. Then and there I sensed something fishy about the entire set-up, for my mining experience told me that this was not gold-bearing rock formation. But, since my business was running down cats, not rats, I changed the subject by advising them: "You'd better get your car over the hill before another storm comes." "One of us is going out with it right away, and down to the valley," spoke one of the young fellows. "Well, I'm going that way myself, and I'll give you a hand and ride down to the Green house, if you don't mind," I offered.

They were agreeable to this, so I helped push the jalopy a mile and a half uphill, got a ride for three miles downhill, and continued to Samson Flat on foot.

I used the forest service telephone at Samson Flat to call Art Bullard, asking him to bring his pick-up truck the next day to move some food and bedding to the cabins at Millwood. Joe Dixon decided to stay on at Samson Flat and gather data on other mammals around there. I made a six-mile hunt to the Green house the next morning and met Art at noon. In the afternoon we moved to Millwood and fixed up the camp there.

Noticing that the road had already been traversed both ways by a small automobile, Art, with the game warden instinct, became suspicious of game law violators. I told him about the strangers I had seen two days before. "Bootleggers, I'll bet," he guessed at once, "and probably game-law violators too. I'll have to look them over after you finish hunting here."

Art decided to spend the next forenoon hunting with me before going home in his car. We started from camp at 7:30 A.M., but because of the icy roadbed and poor traction it was 9 A.M. when we left the car. The snow was crusted thickly enough to bear the weight of any yearling lion, but we kept breaking through knee-deep except at places among trees where limbs of pine and cedar had shed their load of snow to pack it harder on the ground. At one such place, a mile or so from the car, we found a blood-spot about the size of my hand. A few long hairs, like those of a tree-squirrel's tail, were scattered around.

"Looks like a hawk got an early breakfast here," Art suggested. Before I could suggest that it might have been an owl that killed the squirrel and had a late supper, Eli began snooping around a tree nearby. Investigating, we found the tail and all four paws of a tree squirrel piled neatly together. This was typical of the procedure followed by the cougar and so both hawk and owl were cleared of any connection with the killing. As we discussed this, both hounds opened up with exuberant baying thirty yards to the south. We could set the time the killer had passed here at about 6:30 A.M., because the unlucky squirrel would not have been stirring from its arboreal bedroom before daybreak. Now we knew that we had a trail less than four hours old. The dogs confirmed this by the speed they maintained, until we came to the sun-exposed southern slope of McKenzie Ridge, where all snow had been gone for a couple of days. Here the frozen ground was frosted over when the lions prowled there, but by now, 10:00 A.M., the frost had melted and the ground was thawing, thus diluting or washing away the lion-scent, except in shady gulches. Add to this difficulty the further one that the lightweight panthers failed to make any visible impression on the frozen ground, and it was no wonder that it took us six hours to trace our double quarry for as many miles to some granite bluffs known as Stony Point. The pale, winter sun was sinking over the western ridges when the dogs jumped the cats from their bedding place among these rocks. One took off uphill, followed by Scout baying at every jump. The other one headed downward and around toward the upper reaches of Milk ranch canyon, with Ranger hot on the trail and telling the world about it. We couldn't tell which hound had Eli's help, since he barked only when the quarry was sighted or treed. Telling Art to follow Scout and shoot his cat, I ran after Ranger, soon hearing him give the longed-for "treed" bay. Finding the male cat crouched 40 feet up on a live-oak limb which overhung a steep canyon side, I lay the loaded revolver down on a narrow deer trail, got hold of Ranger and tied him to a sapling, so he couldn't attack the cat before it was dead and possibly be crippled as Duke was. Now I was ready to shoot the cat, but my revolver had disappeared. It must have been kicked off while the dog and I were scrambling around there.

I searched below the path, but it was nowhere in sight. Next, I raked frantically among the fallen leaves with my fingers, meanwhile keeping an anxious eye on the nervous cat in the tree. Ranger kept baying impatiently, while I kept finger-raking down the side of the steep canyon. Darkness was coming on. The treed panther began moving around, looking for an out. If Art would but hear Ranger and come with his gun.

As I feared, the cat started to descend slowly and cautiously. Faithful Ranger, with his eyes on the game, charged to the end of his rope, snapped it and plunged on to the lion tree. I followed with waving arms and whooping voice. The worried panther stopped for an instant. A shot rang out close behind me. The startled cat flinched, turned and headed for the tree-top again. I looked around. There was Art, taking aim for another shot. I rushed to Ranger and collared him. Art's pistol rang out again. The panther slithered off his perch, gripped it with his forepaws for a few seconds, then fell tail-first for some fifty feet, bounced, rolled and dragged his spine-shattered body to the creek. Art ran down and finished the cat with a bullet in the brain. It was a yearling male, weighing about 85 pounds. "Why didn't you shoot him before?" Art asked. "I lost my revolver," I explained. Both of us searched for it until darkness stopped us. Meanwhile, Art told me that he failed to find Scout and Eli, concluding that the other lion must have looped around and doubled back over the ridge to our side. When he heard Ranger he thought I hadn't found the dog and ran down to shoot the cat.

Camp was three miles away by road and trail, two miles of which was covered with heavy snow nearly two feet deep. Since darkness would be on us before we could skin the lion, we left it there and trudged with cramping legs through the wilderness to camp, while keeping our ears cocked for sounds of Eli and Scout. But the woods were silent, except for the mournful hooting of a lonesome owl, perched in a sequoia tree across the canyon.

Because the elevation of our camp was some 5,000 feet above sea level, the temperature had dropped low enough to form ice one-fourth of an inch thick on the contents of our water buckets in the cabin before we reached there about 7 P.M. It must have been close to zero by midnight, when sounds of dog-wrangling in the other cabin told us that Scout and Eli had trailed us to camp, after spending some seven hours of faithful efforts to keep their quarry treed. Apparently they gave up hope their master would come. Calling the hungry dogs to our door, I passed out Scout's supper and invited Eli in to have his, so he could eat in peace, for Scout was a glutton, while Eli's table manners were a model of refinement.

Art, who had been nursing a head cold for several days, awoke in the morning with misery in his throat and chest and had to go home. Luckily, we had taken the precaution to drain the radiator into a bucket before leaving his pickup on the ridge. The precaution had been taken automatically— one never can foretell when or where any lion hunt will end. He left his pistol with me in case the dogs treed the female yearling while I was skinning the dead one and hunting for my revolver. However, the living cat must have bedded down in some thicket to catch up on lost sleep, for we never crossed her tracks that day, nor did I find my gun, although I raked the hillside clean, down to the edge of a pool in the creek. Returning to camp late that afternoon I found Ray Stephens had just arrived in his car, bringing food and his 38-caliber revolver with plenty of ammunition. Art had phoned Ray about the loss of my gun and asked him to come in and help me.

The next morning we started back to search the bottom of the pool for my gun, but we never got there. In lion-hunting it's the quarry, more often than it is the hunter, who lays plans for the day's work. The maiden panther, still on the loose, made things tough for us when she prowled across the road in Happy Gap before the snow began crusting the evening before. Striking her tracks there about eight o'clock this morning, the dogs made the next decision in a hurry. With sniffing noses and wagging tails they hit off in a jiffy, through the gap and downhill a half-mile to the western shore of Lake Sequoia, along that to the northern end and up the mountain diagonally toward Grant Grove of Big Trees.

Almost in the shadows of the famous Sequoias, our quarry had turned northward and kept to a course, more or less level, to cross the old Park Road a mile above Millwood. She then graded downward for two miles to cross Abbott Creek and over the dividing ridge to Dry Creek. Crossing that gorge, she had chosen to grade upward for a distance of two miles and a rise of 2,000 feet to the crest-line of Hoist Ridge, 6,500 feet above sea level. All along I had been expecting to jump the lioness out of some sheltered haunt among the granite rocks on the face of Hoist Ridge, run her down mountain and tree her near the Mill Flat Creek trail at some spot three or four miles below Millwood, and planning to return to camp with the cat-hide before nightfall. Now, after reaching the ridge top without routing out or gaining on the elusive feline, we began to talk about spending a cold January night between campfires, going hungry for supper, trying to sleep under an Arizona blanket, and breakfasting on snow and ice-water. An "Arizona blanket," be it known, is something you always have on your back. You lie under it while sprawling belly downward on the cold ground. You can roll over on it whenever your belly begins to freeze. However, you can beat this kind of layout by spending half the night gathering wood to keep four fires going the other half. Lay your wood in suitable piles at the four corners of an area 8 feet or so across each way and flop diagonally between the fires. It's not exactly sleeping in a feather-bed, but you can snatch several hours of shut-eye by catnapping between spells of tending the fires.

By taking turns at napping and firing, two persons can make out well enough. The next morning we followed the cat's tracks along the ridge-road, passing an object of special interest which Ray pointed out to me. It was the huge stump

of a Sequoia tree which had been felled in 1892. A butt section had been sawed off, split into smaller parts and shipped
to Chicago, where it was reassembled at the 1893 World's
Fair. All but the topmost section of the trunk was gone,
having been blasted into saw-logs, hauled to the mill at
Millwood and ripped into boards and timber and sent down
the flume to a sales yard and planing mill at Sanger near
the edge of San Joaquin Valley. Rumor had it that some
500,000 board-feet of lumber were produced from this one
tree—enough to furnish material for the frames, siding and
flooring for 100 cottages consisting of five rooms each—the
makings of a small town. In future hunting here I was to
notice the stumps of a hundred or more trees nearly as large,
mute markers of trees that had gone through the mill and
down the flume to be used at home or shipped abroad.

Our quarry led us to the western end of Hoist Ridge, where
she turned off the old road and onto the Rancheria trail,
which followed down a steep spur ridge having a decline of
3,000 feet in 4 miles to the junction of Samson Flat Creek
and Mill Flat Creek. Overlooking the country by twilight,
I began to understand why the lonely young panther had
chosen to follow a course in snow most of the way.

Certainly she was not hunting food, for deer sign was now
very scarce there (this was spring and summer, rather than
winter, deer-range). True she would find good hunting two
miles down this trail, but there was another motive to consider—force of habit. She was taking the only course she
knew to find her lost mother and brother by searching along
the course of a beat which they had prowled together over
and over again, ever since she was old enough to begin taking some meat in her diet—six weeks of age. I saw that by
turning southward, two miles down this trail, crossing Mill
Flat Creek and following up Blue Canyon for two miles she
would close a loop at the exact spot where her mother had
separated from her and her brother for the last time. This
loop took in an all-year deer-range. Even if she killed a deer
beyond the point on which we stood, she would probably

feed and continue around the beat to find her lost brother and lead him to the feast. If so, there was nothing we could gain by continuing on her trail now and losing a day of hunting tomorrow. By that time we might find her searching among the rocks on Stony Point, where she had last seen her brother.

The hounds refused to leave the faint scent until we dragged them away with lead ropes. Going back to a point from which we could see most of the valley, we spotted the window lights of the cabin occupied by the people who claimed they were miners. We headed for that beacon, making the two-mile trip down a rough, brushy mountain-side that had a total drop of 2,500 feet. The trip was hazardous enough in daylight; we made it in the dark in two hours and without any injuries worse than a few minor scratches and bruises. Seeking directions to the trail we knocked on the cabin door. A murmur of mixed voices, masculine and feminine, indicated a hasty consultation inside. We knocked again, and the door was opened by a young woman. Recognizing myself and the dogs, she said: "It's the lion hunter." "Come in," a man's voice invited. I introduced Ray. Then they told us they had been listening to the hounds baying on the mountain all afternoon. I told them we were looking for the trail to Millwood. The older man said: "Wait till I get a lantern and I'll lead you to where the trail leaves the creek. You can't miss it from there on." We reached camp at 9:30, ready for supper and bed after twelve and a half hours and twenty-five miles of tough going. I wasn't worried about being skunked this day, for I had learned the lion's beat, and knowing cat-nature I was convinced that this one would come back to within three miles of our camp—the place where she had separated from her brother.

*   *   *   *

Before going further on this hunt, let me digress to tell you what happened to the self-styled miners we met. While I killed animal outlaws, I bear them no ill will, but human outlaws are another matter. I was glad to see these brought to justice.

You will remember that Art Bullard had decided to check over the situation at the miners' hangout. On the way in he left his car near the top of McKenzie Ridge and was hiking along when, coming around a turn in the road, he met the boss miner leading a donkey with a pack on his back. Art told me the story of what happened: "I stopped him," Art said, "and told him I was just going in to see if he and his friends had been killing deer, adding that I would look into his pack then and there. The miner pleaded, 'Please don't, Art, I'll give you my word there's no deer-meat in there.' 'I'm not taking your word,' I said, and began removing the canvas covering. At that, the guy jumped over the road bank and ran down toward a manzanita thicket. I took after him, firing a shot in the air. The guy dodged under a bush and hid there like a frightened quail. I collared him and led him back up to the road. There the guy confessed: 'Honestly Art, all I have here is two five-gallon jugs of moonshine liquor.' 'I'll just take that, and you too, down to Dunlap and call up the sheriff,' I told him. While frisking the bootlegger to make sure he had no gun, I found a notebook containing names and addresses of quite a number of high school students, whose families I knew in Reedley."

Continuing his story, Art told me that the fake miner, when confronted with this evidence in the sheriff's office, admitted that most of his customers were teen-aged high school students. A couple of days after the capture, several officers of the law, led by Bullard, discovered the still on the creek bank about half-way between the cabin and the spot where the bootlegger turned back with his lantern the night he guided us up the trail. No wonder he wanted to make sure we did not miss the trail, he was afraid we might have stumbled onto the still with its fire going! The officers searched their cabin but the young guys and their gals were missing. Perhaps they became suspicious when their boss failed to return on time. Predatory animals can't help being what they are but human beings can have no excuse for becoming "varmints." It seems the woods were full of human outlaws on this trip. Let me tell you about three other two-legged varmints we met on this trip, and youthful ones at that. It was the day after the moonshiner gave us a guiding light up the trail. We were going down the Sequoia Lake road on our way to hunt for my gun, when we saw a model T Ford sedan parked at a turn in the road. A few feet from it, three youths were squatted, Indian fashion, around a smoky campfire. As we approached, one looked our way; then all three went hurriedly into a huddle. Eying the hounds suspiciously, one sulky appearing youth asked: "Are those blood-hounds?" "Partly," I replied. "What do they hunt?" he inquired nervously. "Mountain lions." I said. Then in unison they all asked: "Are there many of them around here?" "Only one left," I told them, "I've killed three so far."

While talking, Ray and I had been taking account of things with our eyes, noticing that several brand-new rifles and shotguns were stacked against the road-bank, while all kinds of new fishing tackle and camping equipment were scattered around. Something was wrong here. The three kids were poorly dressed and the model T was old and battered. Yet they had some two or three hundred dollars worth of brand-new sporting equipment. I asked them what they were hunting. "Bears," the tall guy said. "They're all hibernating in their dens at this time of year," I informed them. Ray and I had an idea of what was going on; we tried to think of a way to get away without alarming them. Ray was wearing overalls and a blue denim jumper, instead of his Ranger uniform. Although we felt fairly sure the group did not know who we were, we were worried nevertheless about having to turn our backs on the trio of young gangsters in order to walk away. Finally I hit upon a ruse to get them away from their guns long enough to give us a lead so that we could get out of sight before they could get back to the arsenal. "I'll bet I can show you fellows some lion-tracks in that old road over there," I said, pointing to the old road—

a short-cut we intended to follow for several hundred yards. "Let's see 'em," they all demanded, following us hurriedly. Although I had taken a shot in the dark, so to speak, there the tracks were, just as though they had been made to order by the young lioness two nights before. Following up our luck, I told the surprised youngsters that I had killed this cat's brother in the next canyon two evenings before, and would now trail this one back there. "She will probably be hanging around there hunting for her brother," I told them. Then, on second thought, I advised: "You fellows better get your guns in fifteen minutes from now and be ready to shoot the lion if the dogs happen to chase her this way. If you kill her, you kids can have the hide and thirty dollars bounty." "Gee, you're all right!" they exclaimed. Now that they were off guard and interested in shooting a lion, I felt we could turn our backs and walk away without the risk of being shot in the back.

Once out of sight, Ray asked: "How did you know those cat-tracks were there?" "I didn't, but just thought they might be," I replied. "Anyhow, I wanted to get those kids away from their guns." Ray acknowledged that he also was afraid of turning his back long enough to get around the turn of the road. Once out of sight we decided to pass up the hunt for my revolver for the time being, take a short cut to the Ranger Station, and phone Art Bullard to call the Sheriff. To save two miles of walking by the road, we took a short-cut down mountain through a mile-long thicket composed of mountain mahogany and jimasal bushes. About midway through this, Scout gave tongue some fifty feet to our left. Immediately, Ranger opened up with his dependable announcement of lion tracks, Eli, too, had disappeared from our heels where he had been following. Investigating, we found tracks of a lioness and three kittens, all traveling together. The young ones were about four months old, I judged, by the size of their tracks. What luck—to stumble onto the tracks of four lions, especially since they were going our way: straight to the road below and on down that for a

mile or so to a hog-back ridge which overlooked Greeley
Ranger Station half a mile away. Here they turned off the
road to follow the ridge. I hated to call off the dogs, but we
had more important game to corner this day. We hurried
to the station and telephoned Art, who then told us that the
Sheriff had called that morning to notify him and the constable to be on the lookout for burglars wanted for looting
a hardware and sporting goods store in Fresno. After thank-
ing me for the tip, Art and the constable drove up to Pinehurst
to keep watch on the only road by which the young burglars
could escape with their car. The Sheriff joined them as soon
as he could make the trip from Fresno. All three officers
then drove up to within a half-mile of the burglars' camp,
left their car and, proceeding quietly on foot, surprised the
gang and placed them under arrest. All the stolen articles
were recovered at once.

*   *   *

Our discovery that four lions were in the vicinity meant
that my earnings for this month should be $425, if I could
bag them within two weeks—something which seemed like
a safe bet. Ray and Mrs. Stevens insisted that we stay at the
Ranger Station until we had bagged our new prospects. I
phoned Joe Dixon at Samson Flat and told him about my
plans. He did not want to miss the coming hunt, which
might reveal some interesting data on the life history of the
panther family. He walked the twelve miles to the ranger
station, arriving there at dusk, followed by Duke limping
at his heels.

Early the next morning we climbed to the hog-back ridge
and struck the cat-tracks at once. Trailing was tedious, however, because time, frost and sun had naturally taken their
toll of scent and tended to obliterate most paw-prints. It took
the scenting powers and trailing sagacity of the three hounds
and the vigilance of us three men, Ray, Joe and I, to work
out the trail for some three miles in four hours. Thus, by 11
A.M. we crossed the Sand Creek Road at a point about
halfway between the Dunlap turnoff and Miramonte. From

here on, trailing was easier for the dogs, because they could take the cat's body-scent from the leaves and twigs of jimasal and manzanita bushes which grew in jungle-like abundance for several miles toward the southeast — the direction our quarry had gone. By the time we had fought through this for a mile, our clothes were in tatters, while our hands, wrists, faces and necks were marked with bloody scratches and alive with wood-ticks. We were thirsty and sweating too. There wasn't a drop of water to be found, nor were there any signs of deer to lure the lion family on this course. I decided they must have chosen it to find a short-cut to better deer country beyond.

In exasperation I began criticizing the Forest Service for allowing such a jungle to exist. "They should burn it off during the fall so that grass can take its place, providing forage for cattle and deer. As it is now, these hundreds of acres can only harbor wood-rats and wood-ticks," I complained. Loyal to the existing conservation policy, Ray quoted the official bunk about such jungles being "elfin forests," necessary to preserve the moisture in the ground. Apparently the originator of that foolish theory failed to take into account the fact that all vegetation absorbs water instead of conserving it. "Why nothing else will grow here anyhow," he declared. "If this brush was burned off as you want it, we would have nothing but a parched, barren desert." I laughed derisively. "All right," Ray went on, "I'll soon show you when we reach the top of this next ridge. A hundred acres or so on the far side burned over a couple of years ago." Dixon had been keeping his mouth closed and ears open, so far. As we topped the next ridge, Ray said: "Now I'll show you." He did. But what we saw looked like a hundred acres of ripe wheat. Ripe, golden grass 12 inches tall or more waved in the afternoon breeze, while shining rivulets trickled down various gulches; it was a veritable oasis in a desert of worthless jungle, a deer haven for several bands of these animals which stood grazing or drinking. Delving for his camera, Dixon declared: "This settles your argument for me. I'm going to

take some pictures of this, if only for my own satisfaction."
Ray merely grinned at the time; later he told me that every
experienced forester knew the policy forbidding controlled
burning was wrong.

Here was meat and drink for the predatory family of lions
— this deer haven must have been their objective. If so, the
chances were good that we were now very close to the end of
the trail. As I spoke of this, we watched the dogs with intense
interest and expectancy, at the same time hoping fervently
that they would turn downward and follow the fringe of
bushes bordering this deer-spotted oasis. But we were disappointed when the hounds continued following the scent
along the divide leading eastward, past and away from this
feline "horn of plenty." Perhaps they, like the range cattle,
never suspected that such a park-like, animal paradise could
be found anywhere in this wilderness of jungle growth. It
was now two o'clock. It would take us two hours to reach the
ranger station, where Ray had chores to do. This new turn the
cougar family had taken toward the east gave me a clue as
to where we could head them off or cut their trail tomorrow.
In any case, panther nature would direct them to travel a
circuit which was sure to bring them back to the jungle where
we had first struck their tracks above the ranger station.

Throughout all of this I was worried about the loss of my
revolver and anxious to have a try at raking out the pool in
the canyon directly below where it had disappeared. I
attached great sentimental value to the gun, a value far
greater than money or the necessity of having a suitable
weapon to use in my work. The lost revolver was a present
from three special friends of mine: Joseph A. Donahoe, Jr.,
Eddie Hill and Wakefield Baker Jr. Their initials were in-
scribed on the metal frame of the grip just under the hammer
and under the following inscription: "To J. C. Bruce, State
Lion Hunter, California 1919." Thinking this over as we
hiked back to Ray's station, I announced that I was going to
get a rake from the forest service tool-box at Pinehurst the
next day and rake over all of Sequoia National Forest if neces-

sary to find my revolver. "These cats can wait," I declared, "that is unless they take a notion to cross that old road that we came down the other day, before I go up it tomorrow."

The problem was solved for me in another unexpected way. When we came to the road near the crossing of Mill Creek we noticed the fresh-looking tire tracks of an automobile, apparently headed for the ranger station. Since we could plainly see that these were not made by Art's tires, we began wondering who had come in, and why. Taking a short-cut we reached the station and there found a car bearing the Sequoia Park sign. Its arrival meant a six-months reprieve for the family of feline killers we were hunting. The car belonged to Guy Hopping, Chief Ranger for Sequoia National Park, who had been sent by Park Superintendent Colonel John R. White to arrange for me to come there immediately to track down and kill a number of cougar deer-killers. "They've been slaughtering deer right along the road between Colony Mill Ranger Station and Marble Fork Bridge," Guy reported. Then he added: "If you come over right away we can assign a ranger to help in any way you wish." Joe Dixon was anxious to go and get the facts about the ravage done to park deer by lions in that area, where the wasteful cats were generally protected by park rules. The cats we had been trailing would be worth as much or more later on, when the hides would be larger and so worth more as rugs. Anyhow I was glad to have this opportunity to renew my former acquaintance with Colonel White, whose cooperation I had appreciated on a lion hunt there in November, 1921. I promised to go there immediately after finding my revolver.

We had to catch up other loose ends as well. For instance, our equipment was divided between the Green House and Millwood. My hunting car was at the former place while Ray's car was at Millwood. Finally we called Art, who offered to take me to Pinehurst, from which point I could walk up mountain to hunt my gun. While I was doing that, Art was to take Ray up to get his car and wait there for me until the afternoon. I left Pinehurst with a rake at nine in the morning and reached the site of my gun-hunt an hour later. Having previously raked down the hillside several times over with my fingers, I now decided to tackle the water hole with the rake. My first pass brought out a mass of wet leaves. The next one struck a hard object, but only brought out more wet leaves. Now sighting up to the spot where I'd last placed my revolver I was convinced that any object sliding down from there would necessarily have to pass over the slanting surface of a smooth rock at the edge of the pool before entering it. Moving around to the upper edge of this rock I slid the rake-teeth down along its surface and prodded against the bottom of the pool until I felt the click of metal striking metal. Then raising the teeth, I pushed them outward and downward, hoping to catch the gun in this way. I then pulled the rake up along the slanting surface of the rock until my revolver was brought out, hanging to a rake tooth, by its trigger guard. Fortunately, I had kept it well greased with white vaseline— inside and out—which prevented it from rusting during the five days it had been submerged.

A Feline Love Triangle

Other operations planned for the day were carried out according to schedule. Leaving Greeley about nine o'clock the next morning, January 23, we arrived at Park head-quarters, near Alder Creek, in time for lunch. After talking over the lion situation with Colonel White, we decided to drive to Hospital Rock the next morning and hunt on foot by way of the trail to Deer Ridge, following the new road from there to Giant Forest, where we planned to stay at the lodge. Park Ranger George Brooks was assigned to accompany us and to help tote lion specimens to roads where we could pick them up with my car. This looked like it was going to be a lion hunt deluxe when we left my hunting car at Hospital Rock about nine o'clock on the morning of the 24th. While going up the trail, the dogs turned off to our left with noses sniffing the breeze coming from that direction. Following

them for a short distance we found skeletons of two large
bucks hanging over the brow of a small bluff, supported by
locked antlers resting against a black oak sapling which stood
between them. Since rutting season is fighting time for the
deer family, they must have locked horns sometime between
early November and early December. Probably one buck had
tried to horn in to take over the other buck's group of female
followers. The second one apparently horned right back,
until the two had locked antlers for keeps. Of course there
was no way of telling just how long the pair lived the life of
Siamese twins with their unwilling heads locked together,
before one or the other took the fatal notion to wrestle it out
at this particular spot, with the result that both slid over the
bluff to hang themselves over the sapling standing between
them. Partly stripped deer bones and numerous tracks of
coyotes, foxes and wildcats in the vicinity showed that these
carnivorous animals had benefited by the deer misfortune.

Coming to a point where the road crossed the backbone of
Deer Ridge, Ranger Brooks remarked that he had often seen
lion tracks there during the summer and fall months. Then,
answering my questions, he informed us that the lions usually
followed the road from there on to the old park-road and
down that as far as Cedar Creek at the lower edge of the lion
country. This information gave me the idea that Colony Mill
Ranger Station was the best place to set up our base camp.
As we approached close to the junction of this new road with
the old one, Brooks said: "We ought to find lion tracks pronto
now." He was right. A big tom-cat had limped up the old
road some forty hours before. Why did he limp? Well, because two toes had been snipped off his right front paw within
the last three days. This was revealed by blood splotches stain-
ing the snow at the two exact spots where imprints of the
second and third toe pads ought to be. That any animal
would naturally walk with a limp to favor an acutely sore
paw was a reasonable conclusion, even if fainter impressions
made by the crippled cat-paw had not been there to prove it.
"This looks like someone has sneaked into the park and

planted a panther trap in a runway used regularly by this tom-cat," I remarked. Then on second thought I added, "Or else he has been prowling along some one's trapline outside the park boundary." There was no answer to that for the time being.

But we all agreed that "Tom" would do no more prowling than necessary to feed himself while his toe stubs were healing. Now he was headed toward Morro Rock some two miles away, which was all right with us — until we came to the western base of that towering dome. Here our quarry had taken to a narrow shelf-like projection on the steep face of a cliff hundreds of feet high, a natural cat trail which extended for some forty yards to a pile of mixed slabs and blocks detached from the granite face of Morro Rock to accumulate for centuries behind a solid knob, forming numerous sheltered lairs for wild creatures. Now this crippled panther had immediately chosen it as a perfect sanatorium where he could nap on a sun-drenched couch of granite during the daytime and find shelter from wind and frost at night, while convalescing from his injuries. Meanwhile, unwelcome visitors, such as men and dogs, were barred from pestering him, by barriers impossible for them.

It was lucky for the dogs, too, that they could not climb onto the perilous cat-way without our help. If I had then known about all the other really serious wounds this cat was nursing, and that some were out of reach of his cleansing tongue, I would have been worrying over the possibility of his dying there, where his hide, scalp and skeleton would be out of my reach. As it was, we concluded that he would have to come out within a day or two and go hunting for venison to fill his stomach. Then we might catch him on better and safer ground.

Calling from Giant Forest Lodge that evening I informed Colonel White about what had happened during the day and asked him to have my hunting car and equipment brought up to Colony Mill the next day. As things turned out we could not have planned better if we had been able to foresee exactly what was going to happen. Luckily, the cat worked himself right into our plan. He left his refuge early in the night, retraced his former course and came onto the road at exactly the same place where he had turned off on his way to that refuge.

Thus it was that we found his tracks there at seven o'clock in the morning. We followed them for a mile or so down the road to where a trail turned off toward Sunset Rock. So far, he had retraced the course of his upward journey, as marked by the older, blood-stained tracks. But here he had chosen to change this course by following the trail to Sunset Rock, then turning down the canyon side to Marble Fork and swimming that stream.

By the time we had reached the stream bank all four dogs had crossed to the farther side and were casting around in a thicket of deer-brush. Wading and splashing across in a hurry, we had hardly reached the farther bank when the dogs joined together in a tumult of furious barking and baying in the thicket. Accompanying cat-snarls, growls and hissing told us the lion was standing at bay on the ground. Dixon fumbled for his camera while I drew my revolver from the underarm holster and rushed into the jungle with Brooks close beside me.

As we ran in, the dogs went fighting out the other side. Dixon yelled: "Here he comes." We turned back and out again just as the snarling cat came bounding around the lower corner and straight toward us. He looked as big as a horse as he passed by us in long graceful leaps with ears laid flat, long tail held high and the dog pack barking and baying at his heels. The cat turned uphill to avoid Joe. The dogs overtook him and closed in. Brought to bay, the worried panther humped his back and turned around and around while spitting and slapping at the dogs who were worrying him from all sides at once. I ran up closer to try for a shot without endangering any of the dogs. The desperate feline sidled away from me and over to a black oak tree, glanced all around and then sprang high over one of the dogs and landed six feet up in a crotch of the tree. All four dogs tried to climb the tree at once. The cat glanced their way, then scrambled farther up laboriously as his crippled paw kept losing its grip on the tough oak bark. I yelled to Brooks to collar the hounds and hold them back, while Dixon snapped his camera several times. The rest was easy: a careful shot and the cat came tumbling out with a bullet hole through his heart.

As we rested a bit, Dixon lamented, "Oh, if I had only had a movie camera." I could have heartily seconded that lament, for there was action thrilling enough to fit any hunting film. However, in those days there was no practical, light-weight movie camera available, or, I assure you, I would have had one.

Now we could see that our victim had taken a beating from head to toes. Deep wounds marked his scalp and face, while other marks made by tooth and claws on his neck, shoulders and forelegs gave evidence that he had been in a battle royal with another tomcat. This meant that a she-cat was involved. I thought that if we could back-track our victim to the scene of the battle we might "cherchez the feline la femme" and her lover cat still honeymooning around the scene of the latter's triumph, for apparently our victim had been whipped off by a bigger and better tomcat. While we were making our deductions, Ranger and Scout disappeared. Soon a dog fight began in the lion's late covert. I ran in there and found the canine father and son snarling at each other over the remains of a young doe about seven months old. The deer carcass had been gutted as cleverly as though the job had been done by a skillful butcher with a dull edged knife. The animal's liver and tenderloins had been torn out and devoured by the lion, who, after feeding, had bedded close beside the meat supply. That he intended to guard it against any and all four-legged trespassers to the last was indicated by his having made no effort to get away during the fifteen or twenty minutes that the baying hounds could be heard approaching on his trail.

Even after their arrival he had stood off the four dogs until the dreaded scent and voices of men coming near aroused a sense of fear in his wild animal brain.

Dixon wanted to record the cat's weight at death, whereupon we tied my lightweight, tested sporting scales to a tree branch and hung the body on the hook. The pointer stopped at 145 pounds. The cat's total length (measured by my steel tape) was exactly 7 feet, including a 31-inch tail. Since the animal had suffered a loss of weight as a result of his injury at least equal to that of the venison contained in his stomach, we made no allowance for the stomach contents when recording his weight.

Brooks, who was familiar with the area, estimated that we were approximately a mile and a half upstream from the Marble Fork bridge. We decided to take turns at carrying the whole carcass over rough country to the bridge, a task we accomplished in a little more than one hour. We then found tracks in the road which the crippled lion had made on his way to the spot we had first struck farther up the road. Walking along the road toward Colony Mill, the three of us kept a close watch on the dead cat's tracks, which were plainly imprinted in drying mud most of the way. A mile and a half beyond the bridge we came to a spur ridge where a deer trail crossed the road. Here we saw what we had been looking for — fresher tracks of another male lion whose toe-prints were all in place. Comparing them side by side in the mud we could plainly see that the fresher tracks were a trifle smaller than those made by the three uninjured paws of the lion we had killed. Seemingly, this discovery did not tend to confirm my earlier assumption that the crippled tomcat had been whipped by a larger one — the victor was probably only of average size — 140 pounds, or so.

While we were trying to find out which way the new tomcat had gone from here, the dogs began working downhill along the deer trail. Stringing out with Ranger in the lead, they sniffed among numerous fresh deer tracks which spotted the ground for a hundred yards. Suddenly the hounds opened up with the glad news telling of lion tracks for sure. For the next half mile we witnessed one of those marvelous demonstrations of difficult cold trailing, the like of which I had so often shared in and enjoyed on the lion trails. This time we could not aid the dogs, for human eyes could not see the tracks, which deer herds had trampled over the storm-packed ground a dozen hours after the cat had walked there. So we had to depend on the scenting powers, sagacity and tenacity inherent in the hound nature. It was up to them entirely whether or not we were to add another one or two cats to our bag for the day. Step by step, and track by track, the four dogs searched out the lion scent with each hound taking the lead in turn to search anew, only to have Eli step in front each time one of them voiced his findings with a long-held, deep-toned note.

I would say that this slow work continued for an hour before we came to, and entered, a thicket of saplings growing on a forested bench. Trailing through this for a hundred feet or so, the dogs came out the farther side and suddenly dashed ahead barking and baying at every jump, as though our quarry had been sighted. We were taken by surprise to say the least, but ran ahead into the open timber and saw a male lion lying tail end toward us on a bed of dry pin needles between two large yellow pines some fifty feet beyond. All four dogs were now whooping it up several hundred yards farther on. But our interests were centered, for the time being, on the cat lying there so life-like that I half expected to see him spring to his feet and snarl in our faces. Instinctively, I started to draw my revolver, before it struck me that the animal was as dead as a door-nail. I ran up to get a close look. It was a gruesome sight. The corpse was thin and old looking. Its teeth were blunt and yellowish. The head was mutilated by deep gashes. The neck bore many long, deep lacerations. One hip had been ripped for several inches and both forelegs were riddled with tooth wounds and swollen to nearly twice their natural size. A nest-like bed close beside the corpse felt warm to my hand, thus indicating that the living mate of the dead lion had just left it. This reminded us that the dogs had been barking "treed" for several minutes. "Come on," I said, "let's go and shoot the female."

Dixon stayed there to take photographs of the dead lion where it lay. Brooks and I followed the dogs, and found a fat young female panther treed in a cedar. Never having killed a lion, Brooks wanted to try out his revolver and skill on this one. A 38-caliber bullet through the cat's chest did the job without ado. Her teeth were white and unworn. Her weight was eighty pounds by the scales, that of an average sized female 18 months old, the age at which flapper-cats of her tribe reach sexual maturity. That this one was ready for, and had indulged in mating experience, was indicated by evidence of recent activity in her organs of reproduction.

Again, for the second time within a few days, we had found evidence that male animals had battled to the death over possession of a member of the opposite sex: first the two bucks who died with antlers securely locked together, and now the dead lion and his mutilated antagonist.

Brooks looked at his watch and commented: "Three lions within three hours. We killed the male at ten o'clock and now it is one." Then he offered to carry our latest victim up to the road a quarter of a mile above us, while I went back to get the corpse of the old male.

The hunt for this interesting trio of felines was over, but I wasn't finished with them, for they had provided an example which might prove to be the rule followed by the species in their sex relations. For instance, I wanted to find some clue as to why this robust young female had stuck by the fatally wounded, runty old male until his death and thereafter for several hours, deserting his lifeless body only when the dog-pack came almost upon her. Was it because she had known no other mate, and, having had her first sexual experience with this one, force of habit ruled her desire so strongly that not even the death of her mate could break it at once? All we needed to prove that the larger and younger male lion had been the interloper was to find tracks showing that the other cats had been traveling together for several days before the fight took place. We kept watch on the roadbed while walking along it on our way toward Colony Mill, with the result that we found plenty of evidence in the form of tracks made by the female and her elderly mate five days before—tracks which revealed that the two felines had prowled the road side by side for some two miles, while taking turns at playfully chasing each other one way or another across the roadway.

Now to reconstruct the battle between the tomcats: Tracks of the larger one showed he had come onto the road from the northern side by way of the Black Oak Trail, started down for a short distance toward Marble Fork, maneuvered around there a bit, and then turned around and headed the other way — toward Colony Mill. Probably he had scented romance in the wind coming from that direction, for there was only two hundred yards separating him from the fresh paw-prints of the honeymooning couple at that point. Lured by the inviting possibilities suggested by the lingering odor in the double tracks, the lone tomcat took off downhill on the warm trail of the other two and caught up with them somewhere near the spot where the dead cat was found. A terrific battle began at once. Handicapped by age and overmatched in size and strength, the weaker cat finally went down, but continued to bite and claw while his larger antagonist went to work chewing on the under cat's forearms. Meanwhile the frightened female took to cover, moved around a bit and shinnied up a tree to hide among its branches. As the under cat became weaker the top one became careless and made the mistake of pushing his right paw in the face of his beaten rival. The latter seized the opportunity, closing his jaws in desperation on the big cat-paw, crunching off two toes. The winning cat couldn't take it, quit and limped away. The other one slunk off in another direction to find some suitable place where he could rest and lick his wounds.

The female watched the outcome from her hideout in the tree, staying put until the intruder, crippled and sore, gave up the search for her and left the scene to take a lonesome, limping walk along the easiest course to his favorite refuge among the cliffs of Morro Rock. After a day of rest and seclusion, the old male lion came meandering slowly and painfully back to the place where he had last seen his mate, raked together a bed of pine needles, and flopped there to await her return. Following the unerring animal instinct to meet again at the latest point of separation, the female kept watch there and soon appeared to take her place beside her dying mate.

The question now arises: Why did the young tomcat invade the other lion's territory? In the first place it is the habit of every male cougar periodically to explore the lion country adjoining his own territory to find out if his "services" are needed there. If he finds tomcat scent or paw-blazes where they ought to be, he turns around and goes home to his own tabby or tabbies. That is, he does, unless he crosses some love-lorn tabby on the make, or his nose tells him that the resident tom is honeymooning nearby. In that case he takes to the trail of the honeymooning pair until he overtakes them, where-upon he starts a fracas to determine which is the better tomcat. If it turns out that he is, then the loser changes beats with him. Otherwise the intruder goes home to recover and then goes cat-scouting in the opposite direction to see what is going on in that part of the lion country. Of course, some lonesome tabby may prowl into a neighboring tomcat's terri-tory, latch onto him and take him home with her. In such cases, if the pickings are better in the tabby's homeground, in the form of females or food or both, the tomcat takes up residence there, leaving only occasionally to see how things are going in his old home territory. And so it goes with the love affairs of Felis concolor.

I forgot to mention that, when Dixon attempted to photo-graph the dead lion, he discovered that all the films in his camera had been used up on snapshots of the big one earlier in the morning. We decided to leave the body where it was until we could get a new roll from our pack in my car. On arriving at Colony Mill Station that afternoon we found

Sid Snow photo. Cougar treed in live oak near the Pinnacles, San
Benito County, California.

A feline "love triangle." Left to right: Bruce, the young home-wrecker,
the husband, the female cause of it all.

Jay C. Bruce
1932

180-lb. buck killed by a male cougar.

Young cougar who is camera shy.

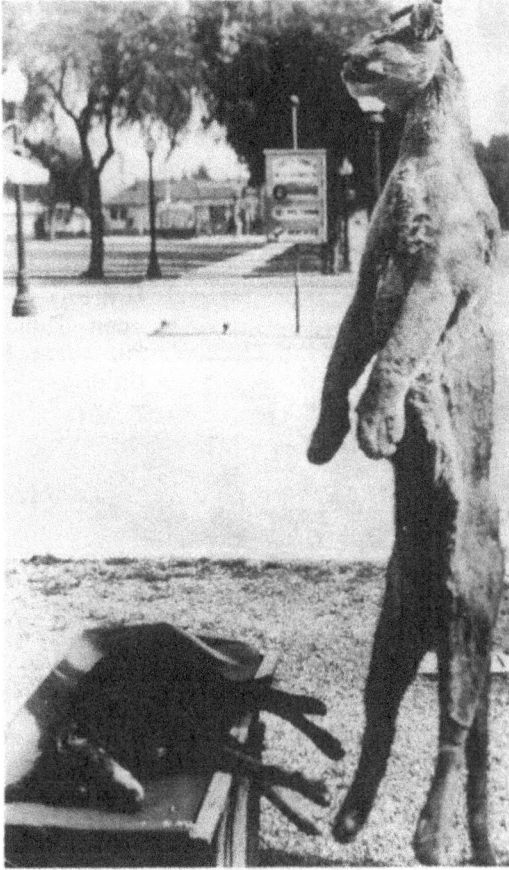

Pete and his slayer.

Skeletons of two buck deer who fought and died with their antlers locked.

Bruce and two of his most famous dogs—Ranger, open trailer, on the left; Eli, silent trailer, on the right.

Chow time at the lion-hunting camp.

Bruce and longest lion taken (7'6", 160lb.).

Ranger looking at a treed lion.

Ten-day-old cougar kitten.

Two hours—fifty trout!

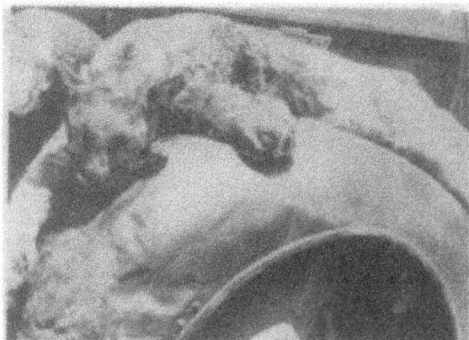

Three-legged lioness—she amputated
her own leg.

A young cougar, last one captured by
Bruce before he retired.

The Bruce homestead in Wawona.

Colonel White and Ranger Fry unloading our equipment there. The next morning, January 26th, I drove out to Marble Fork Bridge and picked up the big lion, while Brooks and Dixon went to photograph the old male on his death bed and bring him up to the road, where I picked up both men and the other two lions with the automobile. At Colony Mill we hung them in a row from the drooping fork of a black oak and took photos of men and cats.

By this time Colonel White had decided to call off the hunt here, saying we'd better leave enough for seed, as he did not want to see the species exterminated. However, he did want me to look over the basin of the South Fork around Clough's Cave, and take a family out of that region. To save time, we moved down to Park Headquarters that afternoon, taking the three lions along without skinning them, so as to show them to the people there. Dixon and Fry took my car while Colonel White and I hiked down the trail and arrived there ahead of the automobile.

While skinning the lions later in the afternoon, we discovered the real cause of the old one's death. It was streptococcus infection (blood poisoning), indicated by the copious formation of pus in the tissues of both of his tooth-punctured forearms. This explained why his weight was only 104 pounds — 16 pounds less than a healthy adult male his length (6 feet 5 inches) should weigh.

Remembering my own experience with old "strep" back in 1914, when an infection cost me a 27% loss of weight during the first month of misery and permanently crippled my left hand, I deemed it not surprising that it had taken 16 pounds (some 17%) off the old lion's body during the three or four days between the time of infection and the lethal results thereof. To me now, that greenish-tinged pus was a warning to handle with care — a warning which I passed on to everyone connected with the job of skinning this cat and cleaning his skeleton. As a further protection, we kept a pail of strong, hot Lysol solution handy to use in sterilizing hands and knives every few minutes until the job was finished.

Dixon was now ready to return with our specimens to the Museum of Vertebrate Zoology and his home in Berkeley. We drove up to my home near Hayward on the 28th, where Joe left me and went on to Berkeley alone. After making out my reports and bounty claims, presenting the hides to our office for cancellation, I delivered the specimens to the M.V.Z. and was ready to start again for Sequoia Park on February 1st.

One Less Cougar Family

Motoring the 235 miles between Hayward and Three Rivers in one day I stayed overnight at the latter place as a guest of the Ernest Britten family. The next morning I drove for nine miles up the South Fork of Kaweah River to the Maxon Ranch, where the road ended, and hunted on foot from there to Clough's Cave — a distance of seven miles by trail. Fred Maxon followed with a saddle horse and pack animal loaded with my supplies. A female lion, a couple of days earlier, had made tracks going up the trail for half a mile between the river ford and the ranger station. The tracks passed by the cabin and headed toward the upper ford near the cave.

Although the misery of an attack of flu was coming on me, there was wood to be dragged in from two hundred yards away and chopped to fit a small cook-stove. I tied the dogs in camp and went to work doing chores while waiting for Maxon to arrive with my equipment.

Toward evening I traced the cat tracks to the river ford near the entrance to Clough's Cave. The next morning I was really down with a cold in head and chest, with no remedy on hand to relieve the misery. Since Chief Ranger Guy Hopping had planned to join me on this hunt as soon as I was ready, I called him at park headquarters and asked him to bring in some aspirin, cold tablets, and some kind of antacid laxative. He came in that afternoon with the medicine.

The next morning we started out the way the lioness had gone, crossed the stream and found fresh lion tracks just beyond it. Farther on we found tracks showing the she-cat had prowled up the trail and down again two nights before.

These regular comings and goings indicated that she had young kittens in a nest somewhere in the vicinity of Clough's Cave. I mentioned this to Hopping. We would have turned around and gone back then to hunt for the cat's cradle, but the dogs had already gone out of ear-shot up the steep trail. The pace was too much for Guy, who kept lagging behind me farther and farther as we climbed. I would have to increase my own pace, as it was, or else risk losing track of the dogs altogether, so I hurried away, stopping only for a few seconds at a time to listen for sounds of the dogs. But all I could hear was the murmur of the breeze in the trees. So long as I could see their tracks in the trail I wasn't worried, but those, too, disappeared a thousand feet farther up.

Trailing by sight would be almost impossible on the grass-covered mountain side all around, but I would have to try it. Turning toward the west, the most likely way for the cat to go, I came across the remains of a medium-sized doe lying some fifty feet from the trail, next to the corpse of her embryo fawn. I hallooed for my companion, but got no answer.

He's given it up and gone back to camp, I thought. Three lion meals, at least, had been taken from the deer carass. The tracks we had seen showed that the killer had come up the trail from the cave that many times, and gone back down it once. Things were beginning to shape up in my mind: She had gone hunting this way, killed the deer, fed and gone home by another route. Returning to the kill the following night she had fed for the second time and gone home by way of the trail this time. Last night she had taken her third and final meal from venison which was now getting too stale and dry to suit her. Leaving some fifty pounds of meat still there for smaller carnivorous animals to clean up, she prowled the deer range, to make a fresh kill on her way home.

Continuing westward toward the limestone ridge above Clough's Cave I crossed a shallow gluch and climbed onto the next ridge to stop and listen again. Not hearing the dogs

I began scanning several gopher mounds and found tracks of cat and dogs imprinted in some of them. A few hundred feet farther along in the direction toward which the tracks were pointed I noticed a drag mark spotted with blood and tufts of deer hair. Following this to the bottom of a gulch below, I found the gutted and still warm carcass of a yearling doe. The nearest high spot was the point of a ridge a hundred yards beyond. Choosing this as a listening post, I hurried up to it and heard all four dogs baying furiously somewhere near to the entrance of Clough's Cave nearly half a mile below. Several disturbing questions entered my mind in a jiffy. Was Guy Hopping there with them? If so, would he try to shoot the lion without first tying the dogs away from the danger zone? Could he save the kittens from being killed by the dogs? They were worth one hundred dollars apiece if taken alive and only one fourth as much when dead. I raced down mountain at full speed, all the while fearing I would hear a gun's report echoing from the cliff below, before I could reach the dogs.

As I descended, the dog voices sounded fainter instead of louder. Maybe the cat has taken to the cave, then it will be just too bad for the dogs, I thought—a thought which spurred me on to greater effort and speed until I reached the trail a hundred yards upstream from the cave's mouth. Then I realized the dogs were close to the cave but not in it. Drawing near, I scrambled helter-skelter over numerous boulders for a hundred feet to approach within some thirty feet of the din created by maddened cat and dog voices. Peeking through an opening between two huge boulders I viewed the scene of action: Under the shelter of an overhanging rock, seven or eight feet high, weaved a snarling and growling cat with ears flattened down and tail fuzzed out big, as she slapped this way and that with widespread paws, armed with five unsheathed claws extended and ready to fend off attacks from three sides at once. Frothing jaws and heaving sides told of a half-hour battle by this fabled coward against odds of four to one in numbers and more than twice her weight in canine muscle, bone and flesh, in a determined effort to protect four bobbing, whimpering kittens over which she stood guard. It had to stop, the sooner the better. My revolver was loaded and ready. I tried to climb onto a boulder high enough so that a bullet fired at the cat's head from its top, would overshoot the milling dogs by a safe margin.

Although her wild heart had staunchly defended her helpless offspring for thirty minutes against four furious canine enemies, a mere glimpse at one specimen of mankind caused her to cringe. Glaring at me with wild eyes, she ignored the snapping dogs long enough to glance down at her kittens as if to say good-bye, while I raised my gun to take aim. Seemingly sensing immediate danger she shot out the farther side, rushed right past the cavern's entrance—a refuge extending some seven hundred feet into the limestone dike—leaped onto a high rock and continued on, springing from one to another, passing over a hundred refuges under or between the boulders until she disappeared around the corner of the cliff's base. So swiftly did she make her getaway that the dogs seemed slow and clumsy in comparison as they clawed their way onto, struggled over, and slid or rolled down boulder after boulder, bawling and baying their impatience.

Fearing she would come to bay in some hidden refuge where the dogs would be unable to escape her teeth and claws, I did my best to keep pace with them.

A few minutes later they traced her to a huge, spreading live oak and began barking "treed." There she lay at rest on a high limb with panting mouth half open.

For a moment I almost felt sorry for her. Then, remembering the expectant mother-deer, whose vitals she had torn out while it was still alive, and the other one killed in like manner this morning, and knowing that these two would make up no more than one fiftieth of the slaughter that would be necessary for her to commit in order to feed her offspring for the first year of their lives alone, I ended her career of killing by a bullet through her heart—a merciful way of dying compared to her own method of killing.

During the last few minutes of action and excitement I hadn't noticed that one of the hounds, Scout, was missing from the scene of the shooting. I had seen him with the pack at the kittens' nest; he must still be there. Three hundred dollars worth of young lion life had probably gone through his mouth by now. Jolted into action I scrambled over the boulders at breakneck pace and met Scout coming our way. Breathlessly, I passed him and hurried to the cat's cradle. It wasn't quite as bad as I had feared, for one kitten was still alive and uninjured. The other three had been mauled and mangled to death—two hundred and twenty-five dollars worth. Gathering up all four I carried them to camp and bedded the living one in a carton. Then I went back, shouldered the mother lion and carried her in. A few minutes later Guy arrived, sore and disheartened at what he thought had been a day of failure. With cats lying all around, that feeling changed to one of disappointment because he had not been there at the finish.

The eyes of the kittens were just beginning to open, indicating that they were about nine days old. There were two of each sex, the male ones being slightly larger than the other two, which tipped the scales at two pounds each—the weight of an adult tree squirrel of average size.

The day of hunting was over by noontime, but there were four cats for me to skin during the afternoon. While I was getting lunch ready, Guy picked up the live kitten and fondled it for a few minutes. Then standing up, he placed the baby cat on his shoulder and stroked it. "Be careful, or it will fall over behind you," I warned him. Before Guy could reply, the kitten gave a quick tug with his forepaws, slipped free of the caressing fingers and fell head-first for five feet—at a cost to me of fifteen dollars a foot—cracking its skull on the concrete floor. Two preventable mishaps had cost me three hundred much-needed dollars this day, but it was all part of the game.

Although this mother-lion and her kittens were in the bag, there was still something I wanted to learn in connection with the hunt for them. Why was it that all four dogs failed to get scent of the maternal lair while we were passing by within 150 feet of it this morning? If this could happen once it could happen again under similar circumstances, and thus might very well cost me the price of more than one family of deer-killers in times to come.

Leaving camp at exactly the same time the following morning, I spent a few minutes checking on the direction of the air current sweeping the maternal bed, and learned that a cool, mountain breeze followed the water course down canyon toward the lower and warmer area of the San Joaquin Valley. Since the cat had located her nursery under the sheltering face of a leaning rock projecting from a massive limestone bluff, no cross-current could come from the north to pick up the feline scent and carry it toward the trail we traveled. Nor could the lair be scented from the north, even though a storm wind happened to be blowing from the south. For any such wind would bank against the thousand-foot-high limestone dike overlooking the spot from the north.

Apparently, Mrs. Felix Concolor Californica had chosen this spot with a view to safety from detection by all possible enemies of infant cougar life, such as coyotes, wild-cats, foxes, domestic dogs and man on the ground level, and golden eagles, hawks and owls from the air. We can eliminate old Bruin, for the time being, because the bear family should be dozing in their dens until the last of March, by which date these kittens would have been following their mother's lead in moving from kill to kill to partake of some venison as they gradually switched their diet from milk to meat.

Her undoing could have been accomplished only by a combination of the two enemies which did it—trained dogs to trail her footsteps to the lair and a man with a gun to back them up. Having found in the air-draught the answer I sought, I continued my hunt for the necessary tom-cat in this case. Going northward up the Cold Spring Trail towards the Salt Creek Ridge, I reached the 5,000-foot contour just as Old Sol came peeping wanly over the snow-mantled crest-

line of the majestic Sierra Nevada Range some 30 air-miles
to the east. Against a colorful background of mottled sky
Mt. Whitney's glacial crest donned a purple cap as the rising
sun drenched its upper reaches—the highest point in these
United States—14,495 feet above the Pacific waves. Entranced
by the marvelous beauty and grandeur of this scene, I viewed
it for the next few minutes, while the purple mantle spread
over many other lofty peaks of the range. Then suddenly
the sun beamed on the snowy, 9,000-foot tip of Homer's
Nose, a snout-shaped knob of granite looming up from the
ridge some three miles to the north of my position. My attention was thus brought to the task on hand.

The dogs were sniffing a western breeze. Looking that
way I counted 29 deer feeding on the grass-covered slope.
A shrill yapping up the trail turned my glances that way.
A pair of coyotes appeared from around a turn some five
hundred feet away, sniffed the air for a few seconds, looked
our way and dodged off toward a thicket, on the run. The
canine honeymoon was due this month, and they were probably coming down to enjoy a wedding breakfast of venison
at the remains of the last two kills done by the lioness, now
deceased, when their keen noses caught the dreaded odor
of man coming from my perspiring body—a warning for them
to seek cover at once.

Coming to a point where the trail angled backward toward
the northwest and a spur ridge took off downhill toward the
southeast, I sensed that this ridge was a natural cat-way for
any prowling "Tom" to follow. But the ground in the trail
was packed so hard that no soft-footed creature could make
an imprint. While I scanned the ground, the dogs trotted
for ten feet to my right, and gathered around a black oak
tree, with sniffing noses and tails wagging swiftly. This was
it. Several mounds of leaf-mold four inches high and eight
inches wide had been kicked up by a tomcat's hind paws
several days ago. Paw marks below every mound showed
that the lion had consistently gone the same way—down ridge
—on every round of his beat. To make sure that any pros-

pective mate desiring his services would not by-pass this turn-off and go down the trail from here, Tom had sprinkled each mound with his own urine as he blazed his way. This bladder scent was what attracted the dogs' noses to the trail-blazes and revealed to us his enemies, a clue to follow in hounding him to death, even though all foot-scent had been dissipated by frost and wind.

Seemingly, Mother Nature had missed her cue when she endowed the male of the feline species with the trait of blazing his trail as an aid to propagation of the race, without taking into account the possibility that every mark he made to guide a mate might lead to his own doom by guiding an enemy.

Now without any foot scent for the hounds to follow, we were able to trace the tomcat's course for more than a mile down ridge to the river, and along that stream for a quarter of a mile to where a fallen tree trunk spanned the water course and served as a bridge for wild animals to cross during times of high water. Crossing on this, I found a blaze near the farther end, pointed toward the lower end of a well-defined spur ridge which extended up to the main divide to the south—the ridge extending eastward from Mt. Dennison's crest 8,600 feet high. Searching out the paw blazes made at suitable spots some three hundred feet apart, I traced their maker's course to the point where this ridge began at the river, and up that far enough to make sure Tom Panther had gone that way. My map showed the trail between our camp and Hockett Meadow crossed this ridge a couple of miles above. Since I expected a friend, Ord Loverin, to join us sometime during the day, I returned to camp to await his arrival, and to give him a chance to get in on the hunt tomorrow. Ord arrived at camp that evening. By daybreak next morning the three of us, Guy, Ord and I, left camp and headed up the trail toward Hockett Meadow. On that shady northern exposed slope, we came to the snowline at 5,000 feet elevation. A half a mile farther up the trail—near the 5,500-foot contour—all four dogs rushed suddenly past us, rounded a point ahead and began baying. Rushing after them, I noticed big, four-inch cat-tracks pointed down-trail in the messed over snow. The hound voices were getting more distant, indicating they were going on the back-track. I sounded several short blasts on my horn, a signal they had been taught to interpret as an order for them to come back and go the other way.

To save time, I told Loverin to find out where the lion had left the trail and wait there until I could get the dogs back. Then, to make sure they heard my horn, I ran toward the dogs and came upon the gutted carcass of a young buck lying in the trail. Other tracks around there showed that the lion's victim belonged to a band of a half dozen deer which had been browsing beside the trail when the cat came along. The cat's tracks showed that he had turned off and taken to the brush on the upper side at a curve from which the deer could first be seen, belly-crawled along between the pin oak stalks to within twenty-five feet of the young buck, rushed from cover and struck the deer down in his tracks. After learning these details, I just had time to notice that all of the deer carcass was there, when the dogs came racing back down the trail in response to my signal, separated at the kill and went to searching for scent amongst the brush on both sides of the trail.

Loverin, who had helped me hunt down two lions three years earlier, knew what to do, so began calling: "Here it is, this way. Here it is, this way." The pin oaks rustled all around, as four excited hounds hastily wove their way toward the point of call. Before I could get there, Loverin's voice was directing them; this way Ranger, this way Eli, and so on until the whole pack went whooping up mountain on a diagonal course towards the cliffs of Dennison Mountain.

Noticing that a coating of ice had formed over the cat's sole-prints we all agreed that the lion had killed the deer no later than midnight.

"The lion never ate one bite of the meat, not even the liver," I told the boys. "He probably had a full stomach at the time," Loverin commented. "I wouldn't be surprised," Guy Hopping said.

The dogs went out of earshot around a corner of the mountain. We struggled through brush and over rocks, trying to get within hearing distance and not lose track of them altogether. A few minutes later we rounded the sound barrier and were happy at hearing hound voices again, some two hundred yards ahead. But they were not sounding the message we were hoping to hear—one telling us the lion was treed.

Instead, they were complaining about losing the quarry's trail in some baffling way, expressing their worry with an occasional long-held note followed by a short one.

Hurrying on, we found them milling around in the shadow of a live oak grove, trying to solve the riddle by going from tree to tree, sniffing the bark as far up as they could reach. "Let's look around in all these trees," I advised, assigning each one of my companions to a certain group while I scanned through a third one. Meanwhile, I kept one eye on the dogs and noticed Eli clamber up onto a flat-topped rock, sniff eagerly along its surface for ten feet to a large live oak standing a foot from the farther end, rear up and place his front paws against the bark. Then sniffing the tree trunk, he looked up and began barking "treed" with enthusiasm.

"Eli found him," I shouted. The hounds gathered around with a rush to join Eli. The other men came on the run, while I drew my revolver and began circling the tree. While their morale was going up, mine began to sink again, for the lion was not there. But Eli said he had been, that he had pretended to climb that tree. Learning this, I knew what to do next.

"We're only wasting time here," I declared. "The cat tricked the dogs by running this far, springing onto that rock and starting to climb that tree, then saw that he had time to double back over his own tracks, and did so, until he almost met the dogs. Then he sprang up into some tree along the way and climbed to a hiding place. All we have to do is to start the dogs on the back trail, follow them closely and look through every tree along the way. We'll find old Tom hiding in one."

The dogs then did something the like of which had astonished me on similar occasions before this: They seemed to have read my mind, or else gotten the same idea of the puzzling situation, just as I expressed mine. Anyhow, they put my thoughts into action before I could begin to direct them by words or motions. Leaving the tree they had been so sure of a minute ago, they took to the back trail all at once, just as I planned to do. In their own way they sniffed the scent, step by step, in every invisible cat-track going and coming for two hundred yards to the place where the fresher scent had been found on their forward race. But no tree held a lion as far as our eyes could see. Baffled again, I began looking around to try to find some possible hide-out we all could have overlooked before. Maybe the dogs had beaten us to it, for they had winded a likely covert and ran to it. It was a natural shelter formed by two rocks eight feet long, having bases four feet apart on the ground and leaning against each other at their tops eight feet above. Voicing their new find, the dogs entered the cavern with caution. We all ran to it and looked in. A nest-like bed of dry oak leaves covering the ground was smoothly padded as though a heavy body had been lying there. The dogs trailed through, checked around and sniffed their way back to the point of entrance. Evidently this was the lion's day-bed, which he had left when he heard the dogs' voices approaching. But what had become of him now? The dogs tried to answer that thought of mine by checking over their former course for the third time, while I racked my brains trying to think of some other way the elusive feline could have turned to escape us.

There was the cliff close by to the south with its scarred face rising up for several hundred feet, and extending beyond the place where we turned back. It looked to be impassable even for a cat, from the base to the top, except for a section

150 feet along, where some natural force had blasted or worn away a mass of granite large enough to form a cove extending nearly a hundred feet into the cliff's face. Looking at it from what I considered to be the viewpoint of a hounded panther I noticed that one would have to spring six feet into the air in order to gain a foothold on the lower edge of the elevated floor of granite at the lowest spot along its full length. Any panther, half-grown or larger, could do that with comparative ease. Having once reached this floor, which slanted upward at an angle of perhaps 60 degrees, any cat could handily traverse its entire surface, from the lower lip to the bluff 75 feet above and lengthwise from end wall to end wall. But looking this over I failed to see the cat crouching there, nor any hiding place for him to lurk in.

While I had been sizing up this situation my two companions had spent those few minutes scanning numerous trees. Ranger's voice close by told me he had discovered scent at a new spot; one within a panther's leap from the lowest spot on the entrance to the slanting floor. Then a temperate breeze, coming from the sun-drenched, warmer slope across the river canyon to the north, swept through the treetops and made me conscious of its arrival by warming my sweat-soaked, chilling clothing. Four canine heads raised at once. Four noses pointed toward the sky. Then all four dogs began whirling around in a sort of war dance, with open maws gasping for air from all directions. What was the matter with them? Were they all going to have a fit at once? We men looked at one another with misgivings. The dogs came to a stop with noses all sniffing and eyes pointed straight at the bluff back of the cave. Then glancing at me for a moment, they made a concerted rush to the lower edge of the up-slanting floor and leaped their highest, trying to get a claw-hold to pull themselves up onto it. Failing in this they ran along the ground below the lip for its entire length and back again baying and barking their dismay at not finding a place they could climb up. The cat must be hiding in some unseen covert near the cliff. With reviving hopes I moved along, casting keen glances at every object resembling any part of a lion. Then suddenly, my eyes caught something that quickened my pulse. "Come here quick!" I called. "Isn't that a lion's tail hanging out of the bushy top of that scrub live oak rooted in a crevice up there near the bluff?" I asked, pointing toward it. "It sure looks like one," they agreed. "I'll darn soon find out," I declared, reaching for my revolver.

Seeing this motion and sensing the excitement in my voice and manner, the dogs gathered to watch my every movement while loading the gun. To be sure of my shot, I gripped the revolver with both hands. Then judging where the chest of a tomcat hiding behind that foliage, and fixed to that tail-like thing, ought to be, I squeezed the trigger. The treetop shuddered as the gun's report resounded from the cliff, and a hoarse cat-voice began an angry snarl which ended in a sickening moan. My friends yelled, "You got him." The dogs went wild with voice and actions.

A big cat body fell from the screening foliage, and came rolling, sliding or tumbling down the steep rock floor, gaining speed until it pitched off the lower lip and landed with a sickening thud between the scattering dogs. The pack circled it once before pitching in with snarling mouths to maul the still quivering body. "Well I'll be darned," someone exclaimed. "I thought sure we had lost him," another voice added.

Now came this question: How was it that the dogs failed to wind the cat before this? Well, there was only one explanation for this seeming failure and it was literally in the wind. You see, that sudden gust of warm, north wind blowing against the high cliff was deflected downward by the outward leaning face until, sweeping the lion's hangout, the cooling air created a down-draft which carried the cat odor with it along the slanting floor and down into the dogs' nostrils. Thus it proved to be an "ill wind" for the lion while it blew some good to us.

After skinning the cat I performed a post-mortem and found five or six pounds of partly digested venison in his

stomach, and a bullet hole through his heart. After returning to camp Guy called Colonel White and told him about
our success. "That will do well enough for this time," the
superintendent instructed. "We don't want to exterminate
the species, but just prevent them from exterminating our
park deer."

This was a sensible program which would tend to make
for better deer hunting in areas bordering the National Parks.
It prevented an overflow of park-bred predators while at
the same time providing for an overflow of deer into those
areas open to hunting by sportsmen. Thus, our National
Parks could serve a double purpose: First, provide a sanc-
tuary for as many deer as natural forage would support,
and secondly preserve an adequate breeding stock of California's number one big-game animals to keep the adjacent
areas well stocked by natural means.

II

CATCHING RATTLERS, GAME, AND TROUT—FOR CASH

/\\

Taming the Wilderness

BEFORE GOING any further with me on lion-hunting expeditions, you might be interested in learning something of my background—my family, my upbringing, and how I came to take up that most hazardous and yet fascinating profession: hounding cougars.

To begin with, let me correct current reports by saying there is no Indian blood in my veins. My grandfather, John Bruce, was a Scotsman, as the name implies. It was claimed by some members of our family that his ancestry dated back to King Robert, himself. However, I cannot vouch for that, nor will I dwell on it. His wife, grandmother Bruce, had some French blood in her veins. Eight of their nine offspring, five boys and four girls, were also born in Scotland, before they came to New York City, U. S. A. There, my father, Albert Olcott Bruce, the youngest of the family, was born on March 5, 1839. In 1852, when he was thirteen years old, he and his family (except one) sailed around Cape Horn and came to California, settling in Mariposa. My mother's side of the family is of Dutch and English descent. She was born in New York State in October, 1852, the daughter of William Van Campen. Shortly after her birth the family moved to Vermont. After farming there for several years the Van Campens decided to move west and came to California in 1860, also by way of Cape Horn.

Meanwhile, Albert Bruce became interested in mechanical engineering, and gave up gold-digging to devote his time and talents to keeping mining machinery in working order and to constructing stamp mills for grinding quartz to free the gold. For several years his services were in constant demand, especially at the mines being operated by General John C. Fremont on the 44,000 acres of mining land granted to Fremont by an act of Congress. There he was kept busy going from one mine to another doing special engineering work, until the mines began closing down one after another. Finding himself without steady work, Al Bruce decided to set up shop for himself in Mariposa and went into the business of repairing guns. Perhaps he had noticed that some of the Colt revolvers were beginning to wear out, while others were gathering a coat of rust, depending on the disposition, steadiness of hand and quickness of eye exhibited by their respective owners. He prospered at his shop until law and order took over, and guns were carefully stored away in greased cloths. The gunsmith business collapsed, leaving its owner with a goodly supply of gun parts and no business, while the courts and lawyers settled disputes in their own way.

Let's leave Al Bruce storing away his surplus stock, while we take a look at the Van Campen family.

As a farmer, Bill Van Campen had come to California looking for farm land, instead of gold mines. Descended from a real pioneer family, he was a nephew of Major Moses Van Campen of Indian war fame, and one of the white men who sat in the last Council of the Genesee Tribe. Having such a background he was well fitted to hew a home out of any wilderness he might choose to settle on. After traveling from Stockton to Mariposa with his family in a farm wagon drawn by his own horses, he chose a site on Elkhorn Creek, five miles from a mining camp named Hornitos (Little Oven, in Spanish), situated in the extreme western part of Mariposa County. There the three Van Campen children rode ten miles a day on horseback to and from school in Hornitos, rain or shine.

After grammar school, Azealia Van Campen (my mother) attended the State Normal School, then situated at Gilroy, thirty miles southeast of San Jose, California. There she took a course in teaching under the direction of John Swett, a noted educator of those times. Leaving there when she was 18 with a teacher's diploma in her satchel, she began teaching the younger generation of Merced County. In the summer of 1872 she taught school in the town of Mariposa, and met Al Bruce. A romance soon developed, culminating in their marriage in December of that year. Nine years later, on September 20th, 1881, I was born at the Washington Mine, about three miles from Hornitos, where father was employed as a master mechanic by the prominent Negro mining engineer and promoter, Mose Rogers. Although I was the fifth child born to them, I was only the second one to survive more than a few months, the first one being a boy two years and two months my senior.

Along about this time two of father's brothers-in-law, Albert Henry Washburn and John J. Cook, were engaged in promoting the construction of a road and establishing a stageline between Mariposa and Yosemite Valley and Mariposa Grove of Big Trees, with headquarters at Clark's Station, formerly owned by Galen Clark, discoverer of those big trees. (My older brother had been named Albert Henry for Washburn. Now I was named Jay Cook, for his partner.)

After purchasing Clark's Station, Washburn and Cook changed its name to Big Tree Station, and erected a rambling log-cabin type of building to accommodate tourists staying overnight.

Since they were long on ambition and short of cash they needed the services of a couple who would be willing to help them get started without demanding regular wages. That couple turned out to be Al Bruce and his wife, the former to design and construct a water-power saw mill and the latter to manage the hotel part of the business.

So it was that the Al Bruce family moved to Clark's Station in the spring of 1882. The next year, while the new hotel building was under construction, the log building caught fire and was totally destroyed. Meanwhile, my two aunts, Jean Bruce Washburn and Frances Bruce Cook, had learned from the natives that the Indian name for big tree was Wa-Wo-Na. Realizing at once that the Indian name was more colorful than the English one, Big Tree Station, my two aunts took it on themselves to change the name of the new hotel and the valley in which it stood — and is still standing — to Wa-wo-na, later simplified to Wawona.

For the next couple of years harmonious relations existed among the Bruces, Washburns and Cooks, to the extent that a cousin of mine, Johnnie Bruce, had been sold a quarter interest in the hotel business. Things were still peaceable when, in March 1884, the stork was hovering over our domicile. Nothing would do but that mother must stay at Aunt Jean's house in San Francisco for the occasion. So it was that our first sister was born at 2525 Fillmore Street in San Francisco.

It still looked like Al Bruce would be a fixture at the hotel, where he was able to turn his hands to every kind of mechanical work, including plumbing and blacksmithing. But a bee had been quietly buzzing under the Bruce bonnets for some months and made itself known when, on April 17, 1884, they filed a claim to 160 acres of land, taking in a stretch of the Merced River and Chilnualna Creek. While their claim would not directly interfere with any rights held by the hotel company, there was the possibility that it might some day provide the foothold for a competing business. My uncles decided the Bruces would have to be starved out before they could fulfill the government requirements leading to the granting of a permanent title to the land.

The first trouble came when father was informed that no lumber would be sold to him, on the ground that it was all needed for the company purposes. However, grandfather Van Campen, who had been employed to help father at the mill, had anticipated this move and taken precautions to save all slabs — waste material — and haul them over to the site chosen for our preemption house, using his own horses and wagon and doing the hauling after his day's work in the mill was done. As soon as this method of disposing of waste material was discovered, grandfather was fired, horses, wagon and all. This turn in events left him free to build our house. So he went to work hewing out sill timbers and riving shakes for roofing.

Then another blow befell us: father was discharged. This meant that he would have to seek work elsewhere to earn money to support us and pay the government two hundred dollars for our land. The mines offered the only opportunity for employment in his line of work. So he kissed us all goodby, slung a roll of blankets over his shoulder and struck out on foot for Mariposa. Going from mine to mine from there on by way of Princeton (later changed to Mt. Bullion), Bear Valley and Coulterville, he found a job at Quartz Mt., on the Mother Lode, some six miles from Sonora, Tuolumne County and 80 miles from Wawona.

Meanwhile grandfather Van Campen had been edging slabs with a hatchet, getting the crude material ready for use in constructing a cabin on our claim. As soon as the efforts became known, the Bruce family was ordered to vacate the old boarding house in which we had been living. Apparently, those in control were determined that no one else should be allowed to get a foothold which might some day provide the basis for competition to their intended monopoly on the exploitation of those two wonders of the world — the Yosemite Valley and Big Trees. Of course, the object was to force us to move out to where the head of our family was earning our living.

However, they had not counted on the Yankee ingenuity and doggedness, inherent in the make-up of the Van Campen tribe.

Mother refused to budge a step until our slab shack was ready for occupancy. Then grandfather moved our belongings to the first home that my parents had owned since their marriage. Grandfather then added a lean-to shed against the back end of the 16x24-foot shack, and filled it with stove wood. Thinking he had prepared us to be able to spend the winter without a man around, grandfather hooked up his four-horse team and drove away in a blustering snowstorm, headed for his own homestead on the bank of the San Joaquin River ten miles west of Merced City — a drive of 80 miles.

Now, in spite of the sense of loneliness affecting her, and the load of responsibility she would bear while trying to keep her little brood fairly comfortable during the long, cold and stormy winter just beginning, mother went about her task with a song on her lips. Right now there was work to be done, and quickly too, for hard, fine particles of snow were already being driven through the unbattened cracks of the slab side-walls while the southeast wind whistled at the eaves and entered through openings between the rafters. Gathering every barley sack she could lay hands on and all extra clothing and discarded garments, mother used our dining table as a stepladder while she tucked the sacks and garments into the largest openings. That done she filled the higher wall-cracks with newspaper while we boys worked at those within our reach.

Many times during that winter those of us sleeping next to the wall were awakened by snow beating on our faces and found a covering of the cold white stuff on our blankets. Three times a week, on mail-days, mother wrapped and tied barley sacks around her shoes and waded for two miles, going and coming through snow knee-deep to send letters to or get them from father.

Most of the hardships endured and troubles encountered during that first winter we spent in our slab-sided shack were indelibly imprinted in my mind. With father 80 miles away and grandfather a like distance from us, we had no man to rely on at home. Neither did we have a gun of any kind for protection, nor even a dog to warn us of the approach of wild animals.

By Christmas not one member of the human race had visited our house to find out if we needed anything. The worst part of this was that we did need something very much, and it was something that any one of several men located in homesteads or timber claims within two or three miles of us could have supplied. This item was fresh meat in the form of venison, which all of them got when they needed it. As middle-aged bachelors they all lived for themselves alone, content with their pipe and a bottle of whiskey for company. Besides these and ourselves the only other all-year residents of our snowbound valley were several Indians of the Chowchilla tribe, living half a mile from us. There was one-eyed Bullock, the camp's medicine man, his squaw, Susie, and her sister, known to us only as Short and Dirty. Other residents were Mary Ann, daughter of Bullock and Sussie, and her man Bush-head Tom. The only children in camp were Joe and Josey Amos, who apparently were orphans being cared for by the others.

Like Indians everywhere, they usually kept to themselves, so we didn't expect them to have any interest in our welfare, or to know anything about the "Christmas spirit," especially since no one of those half-dozen white men gave any evidence of it. As Christmas day approached it looked like this 1884th anniversary of the customary day for rejoicing was going to be a lonely, blue and lean occasion for us at home, and just as lonesome for father eighty miles from home. Certainly, mother felt bitterness in her heart toward those — blood-kin at that — who brought on our misery, through fear of a threat to their potential profits.

Then the scene brightened: a package of toys came from father. The next day two other packages came, one from Aunt Jean Washburn and the other from Aunt Fanny Cook. Now our house was flooded with toys, but still there was no special entree, let alone the conventional turkey around which to arrange a suitable repast.

This was our situation on the morning of December 24th, while mother was still racking her brain trying to think of some way to prepare canned salmon or corned beef to make those items seem less common, when someone knocked on our door. Wondering out loud, "Who in the world can that be?" mother cautiously opened the door. There on our door-step stood Mary Ann, holding a haunch of venison, while little "Injin Joe" close beside her kept shifting his bare feet on the frozen ground.

Passing the venison to mother, Mary Ann said: "Tom, he shoot deer," at the same time holding up two fingers. Then she explained: "Injins think mebby you no got meat for Christmas dinner." Recovering from astonishment, mother invited them in to sit by the stove and talk for a while. Then she explained that we hadn't had any fresh meat for nearly two months, but had been eating canned salmon and canned corned beef.

While our "savage" visitors warmed their feet, mother made coffee and sliced fresh bread she had made that morning. When they were fed and ready to leave, mother slipped a silver dollar in Mary's hand, and said: "You tell Tom to buy some more cartridges for his gun. Then, when you got plenty of venison, bring us some and I pay you more money." At the last minute she wrapped up a loaf of bread, gave it to the squaw and said: "Take this for your dinner tomorrow." Need-less to say, the Bruce family never wanted for fresh meat the balance of the winter, for Tom had plenty of ammunition and was a good deer hunter. Moreover, we kids had gained two redskin playmates through that Christmas Eve visitor from the "Injin Camp."

As for Mary Ann, she became a weekly visitor at our house for the next several years, and learned how to make yeast and raised bread, and how to prepare sage dressing and stuff a haunch or shoulder of venison and roast it. Joe always accompanied Mary Ann and played with us while his aunt was taking culinary lessons from mother.

By mid-January the ground was covered with snow knee-deep and our woodpile was getting low. Mother took to the woods with shovel, saw and ax, digging out and cutting oak limbs into sizes she could drag by a rope fastened around her shoulders. For several days she managed to keep the stoves supplied. Then the storm stopped and the snow crusted over thick enough to hold up mother's weight during the morning hours, provided she carried no load. What she needed was a sled on which to haul the wood. As if in response to her need, Injin Joe appeared, dragging a sled behind him. But apparently he had come to have some fun instead of doing any work. Telling us to "come on" he dragged his sled several hundred feet up the steep hillside back of our house, mounted it, kicked off and came racing down past our door and stopped on a level place close by.

For the next hour or so Bert and I took turns riding with Joe on his *comingi* (*sled* in Indian language). Then mother got an idea. Why not have us bring a load of wood each time we rode down? Joe was willing but his *comingi* wasn't big enough to hold any more than an armful. Mother knew there were several pieces of 2x4-inch scantling stored under the house. She told Joe to get them out. Then she sawed off a couple of pieces about five feet long, while Joe hacked at one end of each piece with our dull hatchet, beveling them to an angle of some forty-five degrees for the front end. Using these for runners and nailing pieces of slabs cross-wise on them, we soon had a rough sled some two feet by five feet in size.

Now a problem arose. Joe insisted on using the new sled, which was a beauty in comparison to his old warped and twisted injin *comingi*. Mother settled that in a jiffy, for it was just to her liking. "Joe is right," she said, "he's older and bigger than you boys and should have the bigger sled when he's riding here." In fact Joe was some three years older than Bert and as big as Bert and me put together. Joe smiled patronizingly and said he would hurry up to the top and load on wood while we took our time. To make a long story shorter, mother cut wood to sled lengths while we kids loaded it on the two *comingis* and gravity rushed it down to our door. At the end of each wood-riding session mother baited us all with cookies and sandwiches. A week or so went by with the woodshed being filled while the cookie jar was being correspondingly emptied.

One morning we were climbing the hill with Joe in the lead as usual, when suddenly our leader stopped, stared down at the snow a moment, and exclaimed: "Look, big lion been here purty soon." We rushed up and saw a line of cat tracks as big as a man's hand, imprinted three inches deep in the snow. Joe began urging us to "Hurry up. We better go home. Old Injin say them fellows purty bad to eat man, same as deer." We took his word for it and raced each other to our house, less than three hundred feet from the panther tracks.

At once mother began recalling and repeating stories she had heard or read, stories telling of how panthers stalked people and sprang on them from limbs of trees overhanging trails the victims were traveling. We were ordered to stay close to home after this. As for Joe, he reluctantly started for the Indian camp, gaining speed at every step while continually twisting his head as far around as possible one way and the other, like a billy-owl trying to keep its eyes focused on some enemy prowling a circular course around it. Apparently, the legend branding this mysterious cat of the mountains as a manhunter had originated in Indian lore and been passed on to the white man, as it had now been passed on to us by our redskin playmate. Joe stuck pretty close to his own wick-i-up for sometime, while we boys never passed under tree branches before scanning them to make sure no panther was lying in wait for us. Mother was suffering from panther jitters, also, and said: "Now I know those fiendish wails we've been hearing at night were uttered by that panther, instead of coyotes, as we thought."

When Joe did visit us again, in late April, he was armed with a willow bow and several arrows, a weapon just about powerful enough to knock over rock lizards four to six inches in length. By coincidence, this was just what we needed to dispose of a horde of those reptiles which had emerged from their winter hibernation quarters and invaded our premises in search of flies. Immediately, Joe was encouraged to declare war on the lizard tribe. Of course we had to take a hand in the fun, with the result that we soon found we would need two more archery outfits to keep all three of us satisfied. Joe selected willow branches from a patch growing on the banks of Willow Creek nearby, while mother found some stout twine. Then, while Joe strung the bows, we whittled arrows out of strips of shakes left over from the roof covering. These went straight for a few feet, but had a tendency to veer off course after that. Mother suggested that we try weighting the head end by driving a small nail ino it. Weighted thus the arrows could be shot for as far as the bow could send them, without veering off course. For the next few days arrows were kept flying and lizards "biting the dust," until not a reptile could be found within a radius of five hundred feet around our dwelling. However we did not abandon shooting with the Indian weapon; on the contrary, we continued to improve our models and use them for practicing on all kinds of small pests, including ground squirrels.

Along about this time mother began warning us to look out for rattlesnakes, since they should be coming out from their winter dens by now and crawl around sunning themselves and hunting for ground squirrels and woodrats. Never having seen a rattler we sounded false alarms several times on finding gopher snakes, whose color pattern somewhat fitted the description of rattlers, as given us by mother. Although grandfather had told us never to kill a gopher snake, since they preyed on mice and rats and were not venomous, mother took the rake to every one we found, saying: "A snake's a snake, to me."

As time went on we began to think that rattlesnakes were something you just heard about but never saw. Meanwhile we had taken a tip from Injin Joe and shed our shoes. When mother objected, saying a snake might bite us. Joe retorted thus: "Them snakes, he don't chase man. Anyhow we run like deer without shoes on."

When we did meet a rattlesnake the setting was all wrong. For instance, we'd been told over and over again that snakes were always found on warm, sun-drenched hillsides. So we felt safe while sauntering down our water trail

one evening, bare-footed and with buckets in hand. Most of
the trail's length was shaded by towering pines and cedars,
while at one spot near the edge of Bear Meadow, a heavily
foliaged, spreading black oak shaded the ground all day long.
This, of all places, was where no self-respecting snake should
be. Nevertheless, lying there crosswise on our trail, was a
thick-bodied snake as long as our ax handle. We stopped
instantly. The snake writhed itself into a coil, stuck its tongue
out at us and began vibrating an upturned set of rattles,
warning us to come no closer. All of which was wasted effort
on the part of the serpent, for we were already backing off
and yelling "rattlesnake" over and over. Mother came running with the rake in hand. Then there began a battle between rake and snake, one which soon ended with the serpent
being virtually reduced to snakeburger.

We asked mother to let us save the rattles, but she refused,
saying they were covered with dust which caused blindness—
another myth generally accepted as fact.

Some Misconceptions Regarding Snakes

At this point you may be interested in some other legendary
misconceptions regarding snakes and thus learn in a short
time of reading all that I learned during a lifetime spent in
the woods. For instance, I had been told over and over by
mountaineers and others that snakes are usually found basking in warm sunshine. Therefore, I had learned to be vigilant
while playing or traveling in such places. Still every snake
I had seen was found crawling or lying in shady spots. For
thirty years I had been wondering why my snakes never ran
true to legend. Then, in July, 1925, I learned by accident
that, to a snake, the difference between shade and sunshine
is a matter of life or death.

I was on my way to Hoag Ranch, where two friends of
mine, Dr. Sterling Bunnell of San Francisco and Dr. Roy
Fuller of Tulare, were to meet me for a lion hunt. Driving

along, I noticed a rattlesnake crossing the road close ahead of my truck. I was carrying a movie camera for the first time, and decided to try it out on the snake, intending to include a scene into the film I was making, portraying lion-hunting in all its phases. But this snake, like all others I had seen, was keeping to shady ground. Leaving the truck, I headed the snake off and steered it toward a sun-drenched spot, where brighter pictures could be taken, expecting the snake to oblige by crossing the spot I had chosen for the scene. On reaching the edge of the sunshine, the rattler balked and turned to one side to keep within the shade of surrounding trees. Grabbing a tree limb lying nearby, I tried to bluff the serpent into doing my bidding, but it would have none of the sunshine, and even chose to brave me and my stick rather than be exposed to the sun. Finally, after considerable opposition from the serpent, striking, rattling and side-winding, I lifted it on my stick and carried it by short spells to a sunny spot fifty feet from the nearest shade and began to operate my camera.

Given its own way the snake headed back toward the spot from which I had taken it, doing its best to reach the shade in a hurry. The time was early afternoon and the ground hot enough to feel uncomfortable to my bare hand; I assumed that the snake belly was feeling uncomfortably hot too. Picturing from every angle, I followed my serpentine subject for some thirty-five feet, while some six or seven minutes passed. Meanwhile the snake kept slowing down foot by foot, until coming to within five feet of shade, it could barely hitch along in a jerky fashion, making but little headway. A few seconds later it began writhing and rolling over and over. Meanwhile, I kept the camera working until the serpent ceased to move except for flopping its head sideways a few times. Then it lay still with mouth gaping wide open. Picking up the body with my bare hands, I noticed that it was stiff as a piece of wire. Considering that I had seen many snakes writhe and squirm for an hour after being decapitated and left lying in the shade, I wondered if it was the rays, or the heat of the sun, that had caused this one to expire so completely that rigor mortis set in by the time life was extinct.

On arriving at Hoag Ranch a few minutes after the snake incident, I found the two physicians waiting there. Dr. Bunnell, who was quite a naturalist as well as a noted surgeon, was playing with a rattlesnake he had captured by hand earlier in the day. I got my first lesson in the proper way to pick up a live rattler with one's bare hands. Taking a short stick, about two feet long, you just spar with the rattler until you see a chance to press its head down firmly on the ground. Then holding it there, you reach out with your other hand and grip the snake's neck between your thumb and index finger, holding it close behind the wide jaw. Now you can remove your stick and lift the venomous serpent off the ground. Not being a constrictor, it will not try to wrap around your arm. If you want to carry it for some distance, just grip the body near the middle with your free hand and take it into camp, in comfort. Meanwhile do not relax your grip on the rattler's neck, or it could nip your thumb or finger.

When the excitement of handling a live rattlesnake was over, I told my friends about my snake dying so mysteriously, without being injured by me in any way. Dr. Bunnell laughed and said: "Didn't you know that snakes cannot live longer than a few minutes when exposed to hot sunshine?" Going on, he explained that snakes are cold-blooded creatures, and cannot perspire to keep cool as warm-blooded ones do. Thus they take on the temperature of their surroundings. Naturally, when the limit of their resistance to heat is reached, they die. So much for the theory that snakes enjoy basking in the hot sunshine. They just cannot stand it, any more than you could survive a fever of 150 degrees. I killed twenty or more rattlers after that just by keeping them in the sunshine of various degrees of heat.

Several serpents, including king snakes and gopher snakes, as well as rattlers, died in five minutes when kept on hot dusty ground around noontime in midsummer. Others, kept on hard ground in sunshine, at an elevation of 3400 feet, where the temperature was 94 degrees in the shade, died in seven to eight minutes. One kept on hard, leaf-covered ground at four o'clock in the afternoon in mid-September, lived for twenty-five minutes. Some two dozen other snakes of different species survived exposure for five to twenty-five minutes, depending upon the time of day and whether cooling breezes were fanning them. Experimenting further, I learned that close to the coastline, where ocean breezes fan the country-side, snakes need have no fear of crossing sunny spaces several hundred feet wide.

Wanting to know how near to death a serpent could be and still recuperate, I exposed them until their struggles had almost ceased and then doused them with cold water. The effect was amazing. The serpents recovered within a minute and began crawling quite strongly. Although they became more mild-mannered and less combative for the experience, they seemed to suffer no lasting ill effects from their close brush with death, and lived in captivity for several weeks, until I put them to death.

While experimenting with snakes for twenty years I learned enough amazing facts about their life history to fill many pages, all of which tend to debunk everything I had heard previous to studying them first-hand.

Woodsman and Hunter at Age Nine

To return to 1885 — father came home in September, grandfather a few weeks later. Both men set to work to make our house more comfortable, and stocked us up with groceries and wood for the winter. About November 1st father set out again for the mines, where he again worked as general mechanic. He returned in June, with six months wages in his pocket, and a woman to care for mother, who, it seemed, was going to have a baby. A new sister was born on July 3rd.

On July 17th, father filed a homestead claim on a quarter section adjoining our preemption on the north side. This took in the Grotto and Chilnualna water falls, two scenic attractions of the locality. To hear them talk, one would think that we expected to live on scenery alone, without any consideration of the five million board feet of timber growing on the 320 acres we expected to own in due time. Grandpa kept talking about splitting fence-posts out of the cedar and hauling them out to the "plains," as the San Joaquin Valley was called in those days, but my parents insisted that not a tree be touched. (Grandpa's plan would have provided a job and an income for father and himself.)

Now that we had the Grotto, our new house would have to be located within sight and talking distance of it so we could keep tourists from carrying away the ferns growing there. The new foundation was laid on a hillside, therefore, instead of some watered spot on a hundred acres of more level land. The time and energy spent leveling our yard would have fenced in a hundred acres of level land.

In November we moved into our homestead house, designed by mother and constructed by father, Uncle Barnes Van Campen and grandpa. It contained eight rooms and was rated as the best house in the mountains. That winter was the worst ever experienced in that locality, even up to the present time. The damage to the nearby hotel and its equipment was considerable. While we suffered some damage too, it brought us some good—father was put in charge of a shop for the hotel company, an assignment that lasted ten years.

Since moving into our homestead house we two older boys had been going to the store and post-office the year around, except sometimes during the winters when snow lay too deep. Quite often we saw tracks of bears, panthers, coyotes, wildcats, foxes and skunks on the road we had to travel for some two miles through a continuous forest. Several times members of the four smaller species mentioned were seen by us at close range — one hundred to three hundred feet. These we didn't mind so much as long as two of us were together.

By the time my brother Bert was eleven and I was going on nine years of age, father decided we ought to learn to shoot. Since father still had the revolver parts left over from his gunsmithing days, he assembled three revolvers, two 45-caliber six-shooters and one 32-caliber five-shooter. Among his equipment were a bullet mold for each caliber revolver, each one having forms for two types of bullets — round ball and conical-shaped bullets. After purchasing powder and caps, our problem was getting lead to use in molding bullets. This we found in tea boxes at the store. For the information of this modern generation, I might mention that nearly all kinds of food came in bulk in those times. For instance, sugar reached the grocer in barrels holding three hundred pounds. Coffee came unroasted and packed in bags holding a hundred pounds. The housewife had to roast the beans in her oven and grind them in a hand-operated mill, usually fastened to a post on the porch or a door casing. Tea came packed in boxes some two feet in size each way and made of thin boards. These boxes were lined with thin sheets of lead to keep out moisture and hold in the flavor. They were made and packed in China and covered with thin paper, glued on, and covered with Chinese writing. The lining of each tea-box supplied enough lead to form a hundred bullets, at least. Crumpling up the sheet lead we melted it in a heavy skillet and poured it into our molds.

Our revolvers, made by Colt, were of the "cap and ball" type — the exact model used by Wild Bill Hickok and Buffalo Bill Cody in their time. Each charge of powder was let to run by gravity into a measuring device fitted to the nozzle of a powder horn, and poured into each cylinder in turn. Then a bullet was inserted by hand and forced down tightly on the powder by a plunger attached to a lever hinged to the revolver frame. Cup-shaped percussion caps were used as primers to explode the charge. These were made to fit over tubes threaded into the back or hammer end of each chamber. In order to hold these man-sized weapons pointed toward any object we youngsters had to use both hands on the grip. Necessity had forced us to find a way to use a revolver almost as effectively as a rifle could be used at ranges up to, say, forty yards. Indeed within a few months we were able to hit squirrels running up trees, and do it right along. Here is how we worked it: Lugging our revolvers in hand we went out hunting with our dog, an Irish setter Uncle Barnes had given us. When old Red struck squirrel tracks, we ran after him until our quarry took to a tree. Then, taking our positions on opposite sides of the tree, we had the squirrel between us, so that, when the rodent spiraled around to keep out of sight of one of us, the other one got some shooting at it. With Bert using the 45-caliber and me the lighter 32-caliber, we kept the pot well supplied with squirrel fricassee — a delicious dish rivaling mountain quail.

In winter, when the ground was covered with snow, quail could be approached closely enough for us to hit them quite often with our short guns. Indeed, the only fresh meat available to us during the time between November and April was that running wild in the woods. Without such a resource to draw on, not even our pioneers would have been able to develop any part of this continent. Still, academic naturalists and wildlife pseudo-experts in general harp on the false charge that our pioneers were wasters of those resources, when the fact is the resources had to be made use of in order for those pioneers to survive — for them it was a case of "root hog or die."

When our original pound of gunpowder was used up, we realized that our guns had to be fed. Luckily we had tanned several of the largest squirrel hides, curing them with a mixture of salt and powdered alum. We took the hides to Thomas Hill's museum, where we were paid one dollar and fifty cents for the three — enough to buy four pounds of powder and caps to explode it.

So far our biggest game had been tree squirrels. One evening as the sun was disappearing behind Signal Peak, old Red began barking "treed" with a shrill note in his voice. Evidently he had bigger game treed some three hundred yards down the Grotto Creek. I remember having no bullets on hand, other than the five loaded in the chambers. Nevertheless, I ran down to the scene, half hoping to find only a squirrel sitting in a small tree. But instead, I saw a big be-whiskered cat crouched on a high branch of a tall black oak. With tufted ears laid flat and whiskers protruding two inches out from each jaw the cat looked mighty fierce. From where I stood, probably fifty feet away, it looked to be as big as our fifty-pound dog. At first I thought it was a young panther and began wondering if its mother was watching us from some place in a nearby thicket, and would take a hand in a fight if I started one. The cat made the decision by starting down the tree. Instantly I took a snap shot at the moving target, breaking the cat's fore leg near the elbow. Spitting and snarl-ing, it sprang onto another limb and clutched precariously at the rough bark with one forepaw. I shot again. The cat fell backward, came tumbling down to the ground, and ran into a thicket, with Red barking at its heels. Within a few seconds the cat and dog were fighting furiously, snarling, spitting, yowling, barking, growling and howling.

Crowding through between the saplings I finally reached the scene of battle, and found the cat bayed against a boulder which protected it from attack from the rear. The furiously milling dog between us prevented me from getting a shot without danger of hitting him. Besides I had only three bullets left in the revolver and didn't want to chance wasting one. Suddenly, I saw a way to get in a shot, or several, with-out having the dog between us. I retreated cautiously, moved around behind the boulder protecting the cat from behind, climbed noiselessly upon it, aimed downward at the fighting cat's back and pressed the trigger. The cat slumped down and the dog plunged in, gripped the cat's throat and began maul-ing it viciously. But the cat wasn't done for by any means, for lying on its broken back it clawed at the dog's head and neck with its one uninjured forepaw until it caught the dog's nose in a mouth grip and held on like a bulldog. Leaning over the battlers I fired from a distance of a foot or so and ended the fracas with a bullet sent into the cat's brain.

Proudly I dragged my first big game animal home, where

mother estimated it to weigh fifty pounds or more. For several years after this, every lynx cat we killed weighed fifty to sixty pounds in our estimation. Later we weighed one of the largest we had ever seen, a male, and found it actually weighed only twenty-eight pounds — three pounds more than average. The largest female I weighed tipped the scales at twenty-five pounds, five pounds more than average.

During the winter following the killing of my first lynx cat, we bagged several cats and about the same number of gray foxes of the common variety. All these hides and those of a dozen tree squirrels were tanned by us and sold, the next spring, to Thomas Hill, bringing us in a couple of dollars apiece for the larger pelts and fifty cents for the squirrel skins — some fifteen dollars in all for our winter's sport.

Even at our age, ten and twelve years respectively, we had found a way to earn a few dollars, while providing meat for our table. At the same time we were protecting the source of that meat supply from depredations by the predators taken incidentally. For those half dozen animals — foxes and wild-cats combined — we killed that winter would necessarily have had to kill three hundred squirrels each year they lived — six times the number we used. (This calculation makes allowance for their getting 60% of their food supply by preying on smaller, useless rodents, both nocturnal and diurnal.)

One day in May I visited Hill's studio to offer some squirrel pelts for sale, and observed the famous artist trying to sell a set of snake rattles to an English tourist. Looking and listening I noticed that in answering questions, Mr. Hill told the prospect that rattlesnakes added one new rattle to their string each year and shed their skins once a year, and that they made a habit of basking in the warm sunshine. Taking all this in I thought I was learning something about rattlesnakes. (How wrong I was, and the venerable Thomas Hill, too, I did not know until thirty-three years later, as I explained earlier.)

The Englishman bought a set of "Buzzers," as he called the rattles, and Mr. Hill pocketed $2.50. Then, seeing me standing there holding the squirrel pelts, the Englishman became interested and asked me how much I was asking for them. Mr. Hill immediately took over and offered to sell them for one dollar each. The Englishman bought one as a souvenir, paying Mr. Hill. As soon as we were alone the latter handed me three dollars and took the lot, six in number, making a profit of 50c apiece for acting as middleman. I was satisfied. Deciding there was more money in rattlesnakes than in pelts, judging by the price the foreigner paid for that average-sized set, I asked Mr. Hill how much he would pay me for rattles like those. "Just bring in all you get," he replied. "I will pay according to their size and condition." Then he added: "If you boys can skin them well, I will pay you twice as much for the skins with rattles attached."

Now it looked like we wouldn't ever have to ask dad for money to buy powder, caps and lead for our "shootin' irons." There was something else we wanted too — a harmonica apiece, things which had to be purchased in Raymond, and could be gotten through the courtesy of any stage driver.

During the summer we tracked down every rattlesnake that was unfortunate enough to cross our road, besides several others found lying in wait within striking distance of burrows inhabited by ground squirrels — their principal prey. On one of these snake hunts, old Red, who accompanied us everywhere, discovered and bayed a huge rattler under the edge of a big log. Luckily, one of us managed to get the business end of our willow snakestick on the venomous head before Red could take hold himself. While skinning the rattler we found two half-grown squirrels in the snake's stomach, both of which appeared to have been swallowed no more than a few hours previously.

After taking part in this killing, Red became a confirmed snake dog, and took to the serpent trails with as much determination as we did. This helped us a lot but also had its drawbacks, since we had to keep a rope leash on him for his own protection. Meanwhile, we had discovered how to identify rattlesnake tracks at once. For instance, the rattlesnake's belly is nearer flat than that of any non-venomous kind, such as the bullsnake (gopher snake) and the king snake. This difference in shape is impressed in dust or soft earth crawled over by any snake. Furthermore, the angularity of rattlesnake tracks is more pronounced than that of other species native to our locality. Another thing we learned was that our largest non-venomous snake is no more than one inch thick — less than half the thickness of a big rattler, although the former may be half as much longer than the latter. With this knowledge to go on we knew at a glance that any snake track more than one inch wide was made by a rattler.

After skinning a couple of our largest victims and being paid only one dollar apiece for their skin and rattles, we struck against doing any more skinning in the true sense, and sneaked a page out of Pike's snake book, so to speak. Who was Pike? Well, he was a picturesque, good-natured, elderly Missourian, of medium stature physically, and sandy complexion. He wore a mustache and goatee, along with hair down to his shoulders, à la Buffalo Bill. His real name was Nathaniel Phillips. He had gained the nickname, Pike, because of his frequent references to Pike County, where he was born. Sometime during his life he had suffered an attack of pneumonia, which had left his vocal cords hardened, so that he could not speak above a hoarse whisper. All in all he was one of the interesting characters of the times and locality. Having served as a guide during the early days of travel into Yosemite by saddle train, he was connected with many colorful events which furnished material for local stories, orally told, but never written. While he preferred to work on the road with pick and shovel, he was capable of jehuing a coach-and-four as safely as any regular stage-driver, and was called on to do so in emergencies.

One of his hobbies was fiddling, six-inch fiddling, which he did by gripping the middle of a home-made bow consisting of a bowed willow stick strung with black hair pulled from the tail of the local stage horses. His favorite tunes were, "Arkansas Traveler," "The Devil's Dream," "Old Zip Coon," and "Ten Little Injins and One Old Squaw." His other hobby was hunting rattlesnakes and splicing together two or more sets of rattles to make the combination look like one unnaturally long string. These he sold to unsuspecting tourists, either directly when he was driving stage, or through other stage-drivers, who sent customers to him.

I seem to have gone "a long way around Robin Hood's barn" before getting to the story I started out to tell you. So here it is. One afternoon I happened to be playing around on the store porch looking for some mischief to get into, when Pike came down from his room in the store attic, sat down on his bed made on the west porch, and began matching several sets of rattles, as to color. Curious, I asked what he was doing. In his hoarse whisper he replied: "I'm just fixing up some rattles for John Bull." For the next half hour I watched him splice together two sets of rattles to make one taken from a large snake look like it should have been if none had been broken off. For instance, a perfect set of rattles would contain every button nature had added, beginning with the first one grown, which would be no more than one quarter of an inch wide. Thereafter, each rattle added would be as much wider and thicker as the snake's tail end had grown in the meantime. Thus, by the time an average rattler had grown twenty buttons, the latest one grown should be about five-eighths of an inch wide and the whole string should be gradually tapered down to one-quarter inch in width at the tip.

Pike's purpose was to make each broken string look like it was a perfect one, by adding a smaller, perfect string containing as many rattles as had apparently been broken or worn off one way or another during the snake's lifetime. In a way this wasn't cheating, but was merely repairing the damage done by the snake's own actions. Personally, I have never found a string containing more than fourteen rattles, and then only once. And judging by the width of the tip end of those, I would say that eight to ten buttons had been lost from that string.

Pike spliced the rattles by forcing the largest button of the smaller string over the smallest button of the larger string. Spliced thus the joint held together as strongly as those nature had put together. When finished, he had a perfect tapered string containing twenty rattles. Slipping them into the side-pocket of his denim jumper, he went around to the front porch and sat on a bench. Soon the stage company superintendent, Tom Martin, started from the hotel accompanied by a tall, dignified-looking tourist. Seeing them coming, Pike warned me thus: "Now Jay, don't you say a word when I talk to that man with Tom." A minute later, Tom Martin was introducing his companion, an Englishman, to Pike and telling the former that Pike was the man who might have some snake rattles to sell. Pike stood up, unloaded a quid of tobacco from his mouth, spat a couple of times and whispered hoarsely: "Too bad I didn't know you wanted some a couple of days ago, for I killed the biggest rattler I ever saw."

Tom Martin asked: "How long was the snake, Pike?" Pike, stretching out both arms to their full length, replied: "About so long."

"How many buzzers did the serpent contain?" asked the Englishman.

"All rattles but his head, by golly," rasped Pike.

"Good Heavens, man!" exclaimed the Englishman. "I will pay you well for those rattlers."

For a moment it looked like Pike was caught in his own trap. But after stamping around for a few moments and spitting a couple of times, he rose to the occasion by replying: "The dang thing jumped at me and hooked his fangs in my pant's leg, so I had to stomp him to death and busted all his rattles except twenty on the end of the string. Here they are, you can have them for twenty dollars." The Englishman counted the rattles, passed a twenty-dollar gold coin to Pike and went up to have dinner at the hotel. Pike went into the barroom and called to a dozen men lounging there, saying: "Everyone come up and have a drink on John Bull."

I'll admit we resorted to Pike's method of increasing the value of snake rattles on several occasions, and were doing all right until mother got wise and forbade us to "cheat" any more. From the first she had been worrying over our handling the revolvers, and still more after we began trailing rattlesnakes. However, we managed to sneak away and find a rattlesnake often enough to keep us supplied with money to buy powder and caps. This was especially true on cloudy days, for we had noticed that snakes were out hunting for food all day when the sky was overcast, while on sunny days they crawled mostly during the hours between sundown and dark. Those found moving earlier in the day kept to shaded areas. Never did we find a snake coiled or stretched out in a sunny spot.

Along toward Fall something happened which we had feared ever since Red took up snake hunting with us. He found a rattler when we weren't with him, and began fighting it at once. Mother, hearing him barking around a big oak, a stone's throw from our back door, stepped out to listen. There was no mistaking that keen, buzzing sound mixed with the dog's voice. "Red's fighting a rattlesnake," she screamed: "Go and help him quick."

I ran, picking up stones as I went. The dog kept sparring with the serpent, which kept striking right back, without either one getting a hold until I came close and hurled a stone at the writhing snake. Red taking this as the signal for him to attack in earnest, leaped at the snake, took hold and began shaking it as he would do to a squirrel. The next instant he yelped and leaped backward, dragging the rattler hooked onto his jaw. Shaking the snake loose, Red ran to the Grotto Creek to cool off in a pool, while I pounded the snake to death with stones. If we had then known that we should have lanced the fang wounds at once and let the blood wash out the venom before it could be carried through the arteries and heart, the dog would probably not have suffered any serious consequences. As it was, all we thought of was washing the wounds with ammonia.

For the next ten days Red was a very sick dog, but thereafter seemed to be recovering, until after a month of lying around, he was ready to go hunting again. However he seemed to sense that he never again would be the same dog when it came to having vim and stamina, and responded listlessly to any call for action. November came with its frosty nights and chilling days and Red seemed content to crawl under the house to sleep in a dry spot directly beneath our living room stove, where he could hear us moving and talking close above him. Then one morning, he failed to appear for breakfast, and was still absent by nightfall. The next morning he was still missing. Fearing the worst, we boys crawled under the house and wormed our way up to the dog's bed. There lay his body stiff and cold. We dragged it out, wrapped it in a shroud of burlap and buried our lost hunting pal three feet deep in a grave we dug next to a natural granite headstone standing within plain view of our living-room door.

All the Trout You Can Eat

The following fourth of July (1894), I was carelessly celebrating with some homemade bombs, foolishly picking up one that I thought was not going to explode. It did — blasting my hands and face with fragments of copper. Although my father did his best to extract the pieces, many remained imbedded even to this day. Two weeks after the accident, my wounds were healed but my fingers were stiff and both hands very tender. Father hired an Indian to cut up enough stove wood to last us for a month. I could have gone to school, but I had another idea in mind — going fishing. I persuaded mother that I couldn't possibly hold a book or pencil for some time to come, although I did manage to hold a willow pole and cast with it.

Now freed of chores and school I began concentrating on fooling and hooking trout, catching five to ten during an afternoon for the first few days. Meanwhile, I had learned that trout are wary of anything that looks unnatural, such as a white shirt or glistening straw hat worn by a person. This I learned by wearing such an outfit one afternoon and noticing that I couldn't get to within casting distance of where the fish were lying before they took off for some deeper waters or hid under rocks. That afternoon I went home with only a few small ones, five to six inches long, in my home-made, denim creel, which mother had made out of an old pair of overalls. Another thing I learned was that a fly of one color — brown — appealed to all the trout more than any light or multicolored fly. A governor or dark brown hackle meets these requirements, provided you nip the tail off them, and trim the wing part back so it is shorter than the feathers on the hook side.

Later on I will explain the reason for mutilating perfectly good-looking, professionally tied flies, and give you a trout's eyeview of them, before and after. I will also tell you how to construct and tie a more durable, and trout-pleasing fly in one minute, by using a dark-brown chicken feather, tying it with a bit of number fifty black thread and trimming it with your teeth.

By observing the above precaution, especially wearing clothes that blend with the foliage on stream banks, I increased my average catch to fifty trout, six to ten inches in length, for an afternoon of sport and did this within two weeks while handicapped with crippled hands. Whereas formerly a mess of trout purchased from a Indian for 25 cents a pound was an uncommon luxury, now we had plenty of trout every morning, with some left over for lunch or supper.

So far our financial gain from my piscatorial exploits had been the money saved on the meat bill. Then, one afternoon I was whipping the rippling waters of the South Fork, and having better luck than usual, when, looking upstream ahead,

I saw a white-coated man wearing a shiny straw hat, standing on a rock in midstream, wielding a glistening rod, equipped with shining ferrules, and a flashing reel. I approached the "de luxe" fisherman, a man about fifty years old, and asked: "How's the fishing?" "No good," he replied, "There aren't any trout in this stream."

"What makes you think so?" I asked cockily. "I haven't caught any, and I've been fishing for the last half hour," he replied. Then noticing my crooked willow pole without any reel, he said, "You don't expect to catch any fish with that rig, do you?" Pretending nonchalance, I replied casually, "Well, I've only got about fifty so far this afternoon." "Fifty!" he exclaimed, jumping off his rocky perch in a hurry and fast stepping from stone to stone to where I stood on the bank. "I'd like to see those trout." After looking into my bag in amazement, he examined my fly and three-foot leader, and said, "That fly of yours is about worn out, let me give you a good one." "No," I said. "It's almost new, but I chewed the feathers off to make it look this way." "But why do you want to spoil a good fly like that?" he replied. "So it will look good to the fish," I replied. He couldn't understand this and said: "Are you trying to tell me that any fish is foolish enough to bite at that dilapidated thing when they won't bite any of these three perfect flies I have on my line?" "Well," I said. "I've caught twenty or more of these in the last half hour and you say you haven't caught even one." To this he challenged, "Let me see you catch one anywhere around here."

It was a good spot on the stream, shaded as it was by tall alders along the southwestern bank, but still I felt nervous at being on the spot and not knowing whether he had already frightened all the fish in the water. However, I crossed to the farther bank, cast in and pulled out an eight-inch trout, which I threw across to the doubter. Within the next five minutes I had hooked five more, between six and nine inches long. In the meantime my new acquaintance had crossed over to my side and was taking mental notes of my actions.

When I was ready to go home, he asked my name and made this proposition: "How would you like to earn five dollars by meeting me here tomorrow and teaching me how to fish like you do?"

When I agreed to this, he offered to pay me two dollars and fifty cents for the fifty trout I had, saying he would never hear the end of it if he failed to bring in enough trout to satisfy his family. Since we were getting fed up with fish anyhow, it was a deal. I then suggested that he come dressed the next day in dark-colored clothes and a dark hat or cap.

He was a willing pupil, taking off the three fancy flies he had been using and substituting the one I mutilated for him. I devoted most of my time advising him, only casting to demonstrate some point he hadn't understood, so that by sundown he had caught all the trout he needed, some two dozen, while I hooked as many more that he had missed. When we parted he was well pleased and said he would be seeing me again next year. I was well pleased too, for I had earned seven dollars and fifty cents while enjoying my favorite sport during two afternoons. This was as much as my brother earned at doing hard, disagreeable work with pick and shovel for some forty hours, or as much as father was paid to manage the store business for thirty hours. Thinking over these facts, I saw the possibility of eventually becoming financially independent, while making others happy, by guiding parties on deer hunts and fishing trips and teaching anyone wanting to learn how to catch the wary trout.

The one thing I needed to start with was a reel and fifty feet of line. I could make a rod out of a hazel stalk, as the Indians did, and asked mother to order a multiplying reel, line and a couple of dozen flies out of a mail-order catalogue, all of which cost me some three dollars. While waiting for this equipment, I searched through a lot of hazel thickets and cut several of the straighter stalks, averaging seven feet in length, peeled the bark off and hung them from a branch of an oak tree near the house. To make them straight, I used another Indian trick; I fastened a twenty-pound stone to the lower (tip end) of each stalk and left them hanging with the weight on until they had seasoned enough to stay straight. Meanwhile, I cut some inch-thick elderberry stalks into sections about nine inches long, forced the pith out with a stick whittled to size, and had a grip and base for the reel seat. For ferrules to hold the reel fast, I used sections of a brass shotgun shell, which I cut off with a file. After fitting and gluing this unit to the best rod, I made line guides by twisting hairpins twice around a small iron rod and bound them to the rod with heavy, black linen thread saturated with bee's wax. When it was finished I had a home-made rod any "Injin" might envy. There was only one drawback — my new reel was nickel-plated and so would heliograph to the trout every cast I made in the sunshine. When I complained about this, mother suggested that I paint it with some brown floor-paint she had on hand, which I did.

For the next couple of weeks I went fishing every afternoon. Meanwhile, trout had become a "drug on the market" at our house. I did very well selling my catch to campers at the public camping ground near the hotel. In September of 1894, I took on another "disagreeable" task besides catching trout. It seems the venerable Thomas Hill decided he wanted to eat two or three mountain quail each week and picked on me to supply them. He provided me with a single-shot, 22-caliber rifle and five hundred bb caps with which to do the hunting. Now I was in my glory, with a good trout rod and a rifle with plenty of ammunition on hand and no wood to chop, I could live the life of Natty Bumppo — the Deerslayer and Leather Stocking — before and after school hours. I even thanked my lucky stars for that bomb exploding in my hands and maiming them to such an extent that I couldn't be expected to swing an ax. Instead of riding to school I hiked through the forests, sniping quail, doves and squirrels. The latter two creatures, not suiting the taste of the famous artist, always went into the Bruce family pot to be stewed with dumplings. When Mr. Hill left Wawona in November to spend the winter at Coronada in San Diego

County, he presented the rifle and remaining cartridges to me.

It was while I was sneaking to within shooting distance of a flock of quail which had revealed their location by answering my whistled calls one October day, that something almost incredible happened. I assumed the quail answering my calls were feeding on black oak acorns shed from a group of oak trees less than three hundred feet from me. In order to get close to them I approached in line with a large rock which stood between me and the gamebirds. Meanwhile, I ceased calling and followed their calls. Coming to the rock I peaked cautiously around one end, and immediately lost all interest in the quail I expected to see. There, standing within sixty feet of me, were four deer — three does and a spike buck — busily feeding on acorns. The buck was nearest to me, about fifty feet away, I judged. Could I kill it with a bb cap, having barely power enough to penetrate a soft pine board one inch thick? I would find out. Pushing the muzzle of the little rifle carefully around the edge of the rock, I aimed at a spot close behind the buck's shoulder blade and pressed the trigger. As the gun spat, the buck flinched and the does raised their heads. I tried to insert another little pellet, while keeping watch on the buck. By the time this was accomplished, maybe ten seconds, the buck staggered backwards for several steps, sat down and rolled over, lifeless. As I ran to my deer, the does bounded away and a dozen or more quail whirred for cover in every direction.

After removing the entrails, I drew out the lungs and heart and learned that the miniature bullet had passed between two ribs and pierced the animal's aorta close to the heart. Now I found that the fun was over and the work still ahead, for I had to walk a long mile to our house, saddle up old Pete, our horse, find a stake-rope and ride back to my kill.

A month or so after bagging the buck with the pop-gun, so to speak, I became the happy owner of two man-sized guns. One of these was a 44-caliber, 1873 model Winchester rifle given me by Robert S. (Bob) Wellman. The other was a 16-gauge, muzzle-loading shotgun, given to me by Mother's cousin, John Van Campen.

Using these two weapons I kept our table well supplied with wild-meat — chiefly squirrel, quail and grouse — for the next several years.

In 1896, at the age of fifteen, a little over five feet ten in height and weighing 120 pounds, I was old enough and big enough to go to work to help support the growing Bruce family. My first few jobs were typical of the period and the people — pick and shovel laborer on the road gang, farm hand, fire fighter, stage coach driver, farm hand again. The jobs were temporary — geared to the work that had to be done and to the season of the year.

In the spring of 1899 my ability to catch trout began really to pay off in cash and at the same time freed me from the farm job I hated. I had been milking twenty-five cows and doing the ranch chores, a job which kept me busy ten hours per day, seven days a week, without getting any pay at all for Sunday work. Mr. Washburn, at the hotel, lost his Indian supply of trout and commissioned me to catch them for the hotel diners.

During the next two seasons of six months each, I whipped the trout streams four to eight hours per day and caught some 32,000 trout, weighing some four thousand pounds in all. After reading the above anyone might imagine that I was just about exterminating the trout, but such was not the case. To prove this, let me tell you that only 21 pairs of rainbow trout are needed to replace, by natural reproduction, the 16,000 I took annually. The average two-year old female spawns about 750 eggs each season. (This is confirmed by experiments made by fish culturists for the California Fish and Game Commission.)

It wasn't scarcity of fish that stopped me from continuing to supply Wawona Hotel with trout; it was a law prohibiting the sale of trout, a law which would have made more sense if it did not protect the greater destroyer of trout life — the blue heron, a bird which, when feeding in mountain streams, usually devours three hundred trout fry every day, until the young fry are wiped out.

It was on one of my fishing trips that I learned that trout and the manufacturers of fancy, artificial flies do not agree on what looks like good eating to trout. I started out one day with six beautiful new flies, and walked eight miles up the old Yosemite trail to Empire Meadow on Alder Creek, which contained brook trout only. With an order of sixteen pounds to be filled, I began casting about 9:00 A.M. and found the trout striking ravenously. But the hooks I depended on happened to be out of a bad lot. One after another the points, including the barbs, broke off, so that by the time four pounds were in my creel, all six hooks were worthless. Here I was eight miles from the hotel, without any flies and my order only one-quarter filled. I thought of two worn-out flies fastened inside my hatband and started digging for worms in the nearby meadow, using an oak limb as a spade. If there ever had been a worm in that meadow they were all gone now. There was one possible chance left. I might be able to repair one of the worn-out flies. It had been a gray hackle and the feather, unwound, was still fastened to the shank of the hook. I rewound it, but had no thread with which to tie it. A piece eight inches long would suffice. Where could I find such a thread in this wilderness? Suddenly I thought of looking at the band of my hat. It was stitched twice around with No. 50 black thread. Carefully, I worked out a piece nearly one foot long. Then gripping one end between my front teeth, I wound it tightly around the feather and hook-shank so as to bind the feather, hackle-like, for the original length of the body, and back to the shank end. There I fastened it by tying two knots, one with each end of the thread. Holding it above my head, I looked upward and got a trout's eye view of my second-hand, emergency creation. It needed some trimming. This I did with my teeth. When I had finished, it looked like anything but what it had originally been. What would the trout think of it? Anxiously I cast into a riffle teeming with eight-inch beauties. Instantly a dozen of them rushed to get the first bite. Within two hours my order was filled and my lure was still in good condition. In fact my minute-made fly had already outlasted any new one I had ever used. Why pay five cents apiece for factory-made ones, when I could purchase bare hooks for ten cents a dozen, tie on feathers in one minute, using no tools other than those which nature had installed in my mouth. I would have to go to our home to pluck hackles from our two cocks, gray ones from the Plymouth Rock and dark brown and black ones from the brown Leghorn.

After filling my order, I caught a couple of dozen for home consumption. After my chores were done that evening, I took them to mother and made out an order for ten dozen hooks listed in a mail order catalogue. A ten-cent spool of No. 50 black thread was all I needed to complete my fly-tying outfit, one which has served all my trout fishing needs ever since, all over California. In case you are interested, I'll say that I used a fly of one color — dark brown — most effectively everywhere.

With the outlawing of commercial fishing for trout, I had to find a job. It was now December, 1900. I started as a laborer on various oil fields, then became a hunting and fishing guide, supplementing this income at night by — of all things — playing a mandolin at dances! Next I worked in the gold mines (at $2.25 per ten-hour day, seven days a week). Anxious to rise above the drudgery and hard work necessary to earn a living, I saved some money and enrolled in a course at a San Francisco School of Mines and Engineering (Healds). I picked the wrong time to do this, however, for my hard-won education was rudely interrupted by the San Francisco earthquake and fire.

In 1910, I married Katherine Fournier. Although we raised a family and lived together for twenty-eight years, the union ended in divorce in 1938. The basic difficulty was the differ-

ence in the way of life preferred by each of us. Mrs. Bruce
wanted civilization, hates the country. I couldn't live without
the woods. Some of you hunting and fishing enthusiasts will
know what I was up against. How often have you had a spat
with the wife because you went on some hunting or fishing
trip with the "boys"?

The responsibilities of marriage and children made it all
the more necessary for me to earn money steadily. I designed,
built and operated a waterpower sawmill to turn out lumber.
I had partners — and as is so often the case, one was un-
scrupulous. After much work and heartache, legal shenani-
gans caused me to lose both the sawmill and my home. While
working during this period I contracted a bad infection in
my left hand, which crippled it for life.

The next several years were tough. Work was hard to find.
I was beset by family intrigue, jealousy, and the enmity of
some of my former business associates. There was just one
ray of sunshine in the whole dark time — I started to supple-
ment my meager family income by hunting cougars for the
bounty that was paid. In the process I built up a reputation
that was to set me solidly on a fascinating lifetime career.

It was also during this period that I acquired my first
hunting dogs — invaluable companions and helpers. I had
stopped at George Wright's house on my way to my attorney
to discuss the sawmill legal fight. As I approached George's
house, two long-tailed, fuzzy-faced, yellow pups ran out to
greet me with threatening yaps, growls, and snapping teeth.
While I was trying to pacify them, George appeared, called
them back and said sorrowfully: "I'm going to shoot those
poor devils today. They're eating me out of house and home."
"Don't do that," I said. "I'll take them home with me if you
will keep them until I return in a couple of days." This he
gladly promised to do. "What's their names?" I asked. "They
haven't got any," he replied. "No use naming 'em when I
thought I'd have to kill 'em."

On inquiring I learned they were out of an airedale bitch.
While we were talking about the pups they did something

unusual for pups their age — about two months. Sniffing the air together, they looked at each other a moment and then took off on the run around the mountainside above the house. A minute later, they began yapping, "Treed," with real enthusiasm. "They've got a squirrel treed," the old man said. "They keep them up for hours at a time every day." These were just the type of dogs I would need to hunt lions with, I thought.

The pups got their names in an interesting way. I had taken them home and was watching them play one noon hour when a squirrel took a notion to have lunch with the hens in the barnyard. He cautiously left his burrow and headed for the yard to steal the grain put out for the hens. He had apparently done this before and was chased back to his burrow by the pups. This time I looked up from my work at filing a saw and observed one of the pups racing close behind the shrilly barking squirrel, who was doing his best to reach its refuge ahead of the yapping death at its heels. I yelled: "Get him boy. Get him boy." Immediately, my mulatto companion, Jackson, chipped in with more encouragement, yelling: "Go get-em Eli! Go get-em Eli!" Either the squirrel was tiring, or the pup put on a sudden burst of speed. In either case, he caught the rodent within one jump of the latter's burrow and mauled it to death. Jackson turned to me with a wise grin and mumbled through a quid of tobacco, "That pup must be a Yale dog. See how quick he caught that varmint after I gave him the Yale slogan: "Go get-em Eli." This gave me an idea and I said, "Yes, and you just gave him a name too. We'll call him Eli."

After killing the squirrel, Eli carried it proudly to our house, lay down in the shade and leisurely set about devouring his prey. The next instant his brother came trotting around the corner, took one look and pounced on Eli from behind, grabbing the squirrel and starting to run away with it. In two jumps Eli caught up with him. A vicious battle began. We ran to separate them and found their jaws locked together, with blood spurting in every direction. I caught Eli by the throat while Jackson did the same with the other pup. Finally, by choking them into submission we got them apart. Dragging him to one side, Jackson began chiding the pup. "What do you mean by jumping on your brother from behind like that and trying to steal his squirrel, you little brute you? That's what you are, just a mean little brute." Then turning to me again, Jackson suggested: "What you say we call this one Brute? It just fits him."

Another interesting sidelight during this period of my life is worth describing here. I had gotten a job as a guide-lecturer for a tourist concession at Mariposa Grove of Big Trees.

Using information I had obtained from my experiences in the woods, I worked up a sort of lecture to keep tourists entertained while they waited for the stage to leave. This actually created an interest which greatly increased the sales of souvenirs.

Among our stock of souvenirs were two walking sticks made of manzanita wood, which Baxter, my employer, had taken on consignment several years before and kept on hand. He had no money tied up in them, and was to get 25% of the sales price if and when they were sold. One, 36 inches long, was priced at forty dollars; and the other one, 42 inches long, bore a price tag marked eighty dollars. Several times during the first month I worked there, Baxter had threatened to pack them up and send them back to their maker in Santa Barbara.

One day, a passenger on one of the stages came in the cabin to look over our stock, spotted the walking sticks, looked at the price tags and asked why they were so expensive. On being told that they were a curiosity because the Smithsonian Institute had a standing offer of five thousand dollars for anyone who could find them a straight piece of manzanita sixty inches long, our customer passed out forty dollars and walked away with the 36-inch stick. A few minutes later he returned and selected a collection of useful items, such as nut bowls, candlesticks, etc., and asked if I could mail them to New York for him. I told him we could. He passed me his card and said: "Just mail the package to this address." I looked at the card and read the name: "Bernard M. Baruch."

A few days later a giant of a man looking for souvenirs spotted the remaining manzanita stick, glanced at the price tag and wanted to know if it was made of gold, or what. Of course I gave him the old sales talk about the five thousand dollars reward. Without batting an eye the big boy passed over eighty bucks and walked out brandishing his brittle stick. A moment later several of his fellow passengers rushed up to me and asked: "Do you know who that man is that bought that cane? That was Diamond Jim Brady."

Well, we were well rid of those sticks of manzanita, and two prominent men seemed happy to have gotten them. At that, they were something unusual.

LIONS KEEP THE WOLF FROM OUR DOOR

/\.∧

Eli and I on Our First Lion Hunt

THE WINTER OF 1915 brought our third child, the end of my job with Baxter and the return of the perennial problem of earning a living. The five of us arrived home in mid-afternoon of December 1 with the proverbial wolf on our trail and due to overtake us soon unless Eli and I could cash in on a couple of lions without delay. However, we were not worried by one problem confronting the present-day family when short of cash — the high cost of meat — for there was an ample supply of deer in the woods and I had a good carbine, two sharp eyes and one uninjured hand to use in bringing home the venison. Our main worry was how to get groceries; that's where the lion bounties would count. But I couldn't track lions on ground frozen so hard no prints could be made by the cat's soft paw-pads. I would have to wait for a snowfall. Luckily, storm clouds began gathering the next day, December 2. By nine o'clock that evening the cold, but welcome, white flakes were drifting down in abundance, giving promise of a layer deep enough to make tracking easy by daybreak.

At 6:00 A.M. the next morning I arose to examine conditions, and found the trees robed in white, while a carpet of snow six inches thick covered the ground. I knew it would be several inches deeper near the base of Wawona Dome, three miles from our dwelling and a thousand feet higher. It was not by accident that I chose this particular section for this important lion hunt. First, the course followed by deer on their migration down country in the early winter and up country during the spring followed the 5000-foot contour line extending through this area and nearly parallel to the South Fork of the Merced River, which flowed westerly through the valley to the south. Situated on a sun-exposed southerly slope, this area produced three varieties of ceanothus (branches of the Buckthorn family), namely: Ceanothus integerrimus (deer brush), Ceanothus velutimus (mountain Mahogany), and Ceanothus cuneatus, all of which provide nourishing food for deer during the winter months. Thus, deer could be found here throughout an average year, the exception being winters of unusually deep snows. In addition to an abundance of venison for food, the area provided ideal shelter for all species of predatory animals, as well as winter dens for bears of all sizes. At the upper edge, these shelters consisted of cave-like holes among the granite boulders and slabs which nature had cast from the lofty face of Wawona Dome and piled at random along its base. A half mile below stood a series of granite walls some two to three hundred feet high and a half mile in length. Here, too, Mother Nature had constructed numerous storm shelters for her wilderness creatures, both large and small. The terrain was ideal for both deer and their natural enemies, particularly the cougar. In fact, I had in the past seen more lion tracks in this section than in any area of like size around our homestead. Now I was particularly anxious to find the tracks of a mother-cat and have the chance to bag the family, and thus earn sixty to eighty dollars in one day.

With all the foregoing considerations in mind, I started from our house at seven o'clock in a spitting snow shower, indicating the end of the storm. To prevent Eli from chasing deer or tree squirrels, I led him at the end of a five-foot length of rope. By the time we reached the first bench, two miles from home, the clouds were beginning to part and expose sections of blue sky. After wading knee-deep through the icy waters of Chilnualna Creek, we climbed another half-mile to a spur marking the turning point of the watershed between the river and Chilnualna Creek, similar to the configuration of the hip on a house roof. I hoped that any lion habitually prowling this area had taken cover during the night storm and waited until morning before prowling. If not, all tracks made early in the night would be covered completely, or nearly so.

By nine o'clock the sun came out and the trees began to shed their load of snow, thus brightening the day, if darkening my hopes, for all tracks imprinted in the ground-covering under the trees would be obliterated by the deluge of snow falling from the leaves and branches. This made it necessary for me to proceed by a roundabout course through clean snow, bordering thickets, or covering the wider spaces between the trees, where tracks could be seen. By nine-thirty I was beginning to wonder if I had chosen the right hunting ground. Then, while viewing an open course ahead, I saw what I was longing to see — a line of round holes three inches in diameter and spaced some twenty-two inches apart, down a slope thirty feet ahead of me. I hastened to investigate them, and sure enough, there, in the bottom, were imprinted four toes more sharply pointed than those of a dog, and the corrugated heel-pads of the cat family. A layer of finely grained snow covered the sole prints to a depth of a quarter of an inch, thus setting the time Mrs. Lion had passed here as being close to seven o'clock — the time I had left home that morning. I encouraged Eli to smell them, but he was not interested. This I understood, since the natural quarry for the canine family are the animals they can run down and catch on the ground, such as deer, rabbits and various species of rodents. All those who can escape by climbing trees, such as coons, wildcats, bears, and panthers are usually passed up by the untrained hunting dog. This is especially true regarding bears and panthers, for any sensible dog instinctively knows that those heavily armed animals could make short work of him, or even several of his tribe in a life-and-death battle. But once the dog learns that, with a man and gun to back him up, he can get his teeth into the largest kind of game, even though the quarry takes to a tree to avoid capture, the canine hunter becomes soon converted to the slogan of the wrestling and prize ring: "The bigger they are, the harder they fall." From then on, small animals, and even the fleet, long-winded deer lose their attraction as worth-while quarry. Of course, I am speaking of hunting dogs endowed with the instinct to look up a tree to locate their quarry when the scent ends near such tree, and to bark "treed" so as to direct his master to the location of the game. Eli possessed all these characteristics necessary to make him become a great hunter of mountain lions, bears, and other tree-climbing animals.

Now we were on lion tracks not more than three hours old — probably less. I started to follow them with all the enthusiasm of a hunting panther scenting a deer nearby, but with much less caution and much more noise, for experience had taught me that the chance of catching a panther off guard is slim indeed. Only a dog's nose can be depended on to scent out and surprise this most elusive of all American wild animals. The cat's tracks led us downhill for six or seven hundred feet, then eastward for nearly a half-mile, and uphill on a curving course. At the edge of a pine thicket she'd passed through on an eastward course, our lion had stopped, then backed up for several steps, leaving a double set of tracks over that distance. Evidently she had seen or scented a deer ahead and backed under cover to plan an attack. She had turned uphill to the left and come out at the northern edge, some sixty feet from the near end of a wall-like bluff of granite twelve or fifteen feet high and some fifty feet long, one which, like numerous others in the mountains, formed a barrier holding back soil washed down from above, until a bench-like fill was created.

Looking ahead along the line of cat tracks, I saw something which puzzled me for a few minutes, for some sort of smooth body had been dragged lightly over the snow for the full distance across this treeless area. Suddenly I realized that these marks were made by the lion's belly as she stalked the unsuspecting deer. But instead of continuing toward her victim she turned to her left and uphill for thirty feet to the level of the bench. Perhaps her nose had informed her of what she would find there, or maybe she was as much surprised as I was to learn that her own half-grown offspring was crouched on a rock above, with eyes peeking over its edge to keep watch on some object of interest below and beyond.

At first sight of the new tracks, which were half an inch smaller each way than those I had followed so far, I thought the larger lion had unwittingly led us to a favorite haunt where she'd left the smaller cat while she went on this lone hunt. But after studying the action of both animals as recorded by paw-prints in the snow, I reconstructed the event as follows: The young panther, prowling on his own, had come from some place where his mother had left him, probably some covert situated above where we first discovered the larger tracks. By prowling a shorter course, the young hunter had arrived here before his mother did by her meandering way, scented the same prospective prey the mother was stalking, and crept to the highest rock for observation of the hillside beyond and below. The mother panther, spotting her youngster out of bounds, and stealing a march on her, was so provoked that she intended to punish him. She sneaked toward his lookout and reached the base of that before the wayward kitten noticed her. Apparently, young Tom didn't like the look in mama's eye, for tracks showed that he slithered backward halfway down the rock, then sprang some eight feet off the farther side, just in time to slip past the old lady as she rushed him. Then, without missing a leap, he took to his back-track in ten-foot leaps, with mama hot on his trail for nearly a hundred yards. Tracks were so mixed that I had to trace them for that distance to learn that the old cat had retraced her running leaps at walking pace all the way back to the kitten's rock, crept to the top just as her kitten had done before her, sized up the situation, backed down and cat-walked to the farther end of the granite wall, with tail and belly brushing the snow in several places, then crept outward to the rocky rim, peeked over, backed several steps and belly-crawled downhill, keeping close to the end rocks until she came to the lowest one.

From here she rushed in twelve-foot leaps toward a group of big pines a hundred feet away. Spurred on by the exciting prospect of finding bloodstains in the snow and marks made by a body being dragged to the cover of thickets below, I trotted along the line of tracks in anticipation of jumping our quarry fresh from a kill. But an empty deer bed near the foot of the nearest tree, and deer tracks in bunches of four, spaced some fifteen feet apart, showed that the watchful deer had seen the charging cat in time to spring from its bed when the killer was forty feet away. At this point the cat turned downhill to head off the deer, but a four-foot pine stood in her way. To get past this barrier she swerved farther downhill so as to connect with her quarry as it passed from behind the tree. The deer, evidently a doe, foiled the cat's attack by resorting to the tactics used by the antlered male of the species to block the aim and bullets of mankind; that is, she turned sharply to her left at the tree and raced straight away behind this natural protection. As a result of this unexpected move, the panther found nothing but air to grapple for, instead of the living body she had expected to strike with the full force of her ninety-pound body moving at a speed of 35 or 40 feet a second — force enough to send a deer of equal weight hurtling through the air for 15 or 20 feet to land prostrate on the ground, where the killer could finish her bloody job with teeth and claws. That this one was outwitted by a narrow margin was evidenced by the extra long leap she made to pass by the tree at the right instant and height to connect with her quarry if the latter had kept to its original course.

The expert hunter and killer had lost this game, but wasn't nonplussed; for, without hesitation, she took advantage of her changed position to swerve farther to the downhill side and give chase to another deer — the last one of four in that band to realize the danger and try to escape after the confusion generated by the panther's first charge. Again there was a mad race for life or food, with the frightened deer zigzagging every forty feet or so, and always in the nick of time to escape the grasping claws of the pursuing cat.

After a close race over a distance of six or seven hundred feet, over logs, between boulders and bushes, and through thickets of pine, cedar and oak saplings, superior speed won for the long-winded deer, which finally turned uphill with the long-spaced leaps of a fresh animal. The short-winded cat seemed to have spent her enthusiasm along with her energy and realized that she was beaten again, for she stopped almost as suddenly as she started this chase, stood a moment as though undecided as to her next move, took a few short steps ahead, then walked to the sunny side of a big rock and crouched on her belly under its projecting brow. Evidently she was tired and breathless, but still the hunting feline, lying in wait for any suitable prey happening to pass her way while she rested to recover from the all-out strain of the recent chase.

Reviewing the details of these two fruitless attempts made by the female panther to catch her natural prey, I began to understand that these big cats must stalk to within forty feet of any deer — half-grown or larger — before charging to attack, if they were to have an even chance of bringing down their prey. It might be argued that the cougar, a nocturnal prowler by nature, was at a disadvantage hunting by daylight, but that is doubtful, because deer usually lie down to rest during the daytime, especially in clear weather, and might be oftener caught offguard in the daytime. On the other hand, deer, too, are nocturnal feeders as a rule, and more so during the warmer months of the year. Thus, they are on their feet and are consequently more alert to danger during the hours of darkness.

As I examined and studied the signs which revealed the cat's actions, Eli began to take keen interest in the lion odor, realizing that it was the cat I was hunting, not the deer, whose more profuse odor had mixed with fainter cat-scent for a distance of several hundred feet leading up to this point. To confirm this idea in the dog's brain, I encouraged Eli by pointing to the lion tracks, meanwhile exclaiming: "Here it is, Eli; here it is." The dog responded with eagerness and would have trailed the big cat ahead of me if I let him go. But I decided that nothing would be gained that way, since snow from the trees had covered all tracks and scent wherever the cat had prowled through thickets and close to larger trees, as was the habit of any feline on the hunt. I had to hold him back until we came to uncovered tracks, where man and dog could each do his part.

After crossing Boulder Creek a mile farther on, our quarry followed a well-worn deer trail leading up a gulch for several hundred feet to the upper end of a spur-ridge, lying nearly parallel to the creek and extending from the eastern base of Wawona Dome, downward nearly a mile toward the river. When nearly to the head of this gulch, the lioness had left the trail and climbed for ten yards to a small spur where she could view the area for some five hundred feet to the south, staying there long enough to shift her front paws twice, making that many sets of tracks, as though uncertain as to which way she should go from here. Probably deer scent was in the wind and she was trying to locate the game.

After making her survey by sniffing the breeze in her face, the expert hunter had seen fit to trot with longer steps for thirty yards to the northern edge of a manzanita thicket which extended for three hundred yards down the ridge. While studying the cat tracks where she had stopped to look, listen and smell, I caught sight of a large, heavy-antlered buck deer emerging from the westerly edge of a thicket of pine saplings a hundred yards or so to the south. Two large does and a half-grown deer (six months old) followed close behind their leader, who, being more vigilant, spotted me first, turned and stood facing my way while his mates for the time being, and the latest offspring of one of them, gathered around the polygamous male animal. The rutting (mating) season was in full swing.

During the minute or so I stood watching the four deer standing in the open, some fifty feet from the thicket, with ears cocked forward and all eyes gazing at me and my dog, I thought how wonderful it would be if the cat we were trailing happened to be stalking those deer, and would rush out of the thicket and strike down one of them while we watched. I could run down there and sick the dog on the killer while she was ravenously tearing out the vitals of her prey. But any such wishful thinking on my part seemed far-fetched, considering the odds against its happening without the stage being set by design. I moved on along the line of cat tracks to the edge of the thicket, but glanced at the deer in time to see the buck trotting away with ears laid backward. The other three deer were turning to follow their leader as I passed out of sight behind the bushes.

If I had stepped backward the next instant, I would have seen our panther charging the last of those deer, and the narrow escape of her quarry. But let us follow the trail and read the story as recorded by tracks in the snow. The big cat-tracks led us straight to the tracks made by the four deer. The cat's tracks were implanted in those of the deer for some two hundred feet along a worn trail wending between trees and bushes. Then the stalker had crouched behind a man-zanita bush growing in the curve of the deer-trail. Apparently she was watching the deer crossing an open space ahead, but too far away to be caught by surprise. Twenty feet away to her right, on the other hand, the thicket grew nearly parallel with the deer's course, and furnished cover to screen the panther's movements.

This natural set-up was perfect for the feline purpose. She belly-crawled to the thicket and disappeared into its dark-ness. At this point I became as breathless with excitement as the panther must have been, for it was evident that the four deer I had watched were those she was trailing. She had no more than one hundred fifty feet to go in order to reach the place where her quarry had emerged from the tree-covered extension of this same thicket. Spurred on by impatience to learn the outcome, I hurried after the deer to make sure they had gone into this same thicket. Sure enough, the trail they followed traced the easiest way between the saplings to the exact spot where I'd seen the four deer emerge, some fifteen minutes earlier. But the stalking cat had not made any tracks on this runway, and so must have been approaching at an angle from the right so as to be in a position to charge from cover when the deer came into the open. Then, what had prevented her from attacking while I was watching the deer as they left the thicket? This was explained when I came to that spot; for, there, implanted in the snow behind a screening manzanita bush growing at the very edge of the thicket, were lion tracks and belly marks pointing toward a spot between the position occupied by the deer sixty feet ahead and the position where I had stood before, watching the deer. While this bush was in plain sight from my position at that time, the hidden cat was not visible to me; while she, crouching close to the bush, could see the dog and me by peeking between the branches.

This certainly was her unlucky day! First her own offspring had interfered and worried her earlier in the day. This time, with the meat practically within her grasp, she was thwarted by the appearance of the only creature she feared — a man. In my mind's eye I could see this feline assassin lying in ambush within striking distance of four specimens of her natural prey, with one eye hungrily watching them, while the other eye was fearfully focused on her dreaded enemies.

Fear overcame the urge to kill and kept her from charging into the open until I had passed from her view, behind the bushes. Then she had rushed at the escaping deer in a desperate effort to recoup her loss. And again the race had been a close one downhill over rough ground. And again the long-winded deer had barely escaped her claws and teeth. From the set-up of tracks, which showed that the cat had nearly caught the hindmost and smaller deer no more than fifty feet from where the latter was on the move as I passed out of sight, I could tell that the killer charged the instant my back was turned. I held the dog in check while tracing the zigzag course followed by the deer and its pursuer for some six hundred feet to where the cat lost out. Significantly, she did not take time out to rest and get back her wind this time, but turned downhill and headed toward a stretch of rough country, stepping along at a fast cat-trot, which indicated that in spite of the excitement of this latest chase, she hadn't forgotten the enemies she'd observed dogging her own footsteps, even as she had stalked the deer ahead of her. This was still more evident when her tracks led us to the top of a bluff-like pile of granite rocks and down a hazardous course among boulders resting on a solid granite base more than a hundred feet long and nearly forty feet high. Here she turned toward the right, as though seeking a hiding place in den-like holes between boulders. I moved cautiously, expecting to hear a warning growl any second, while Eli sniffed the scent left on the boulders or in passage-ways between them. It was a thrilling situation for man and dog alike; for either one or both of us could easily be knocked over the rim to death by a charging cat, whether it was to attack or to escape.

However, the cat considered this location an ideal one for the purpose of throwing us off her tracks and to escape to renew the hunt for food. Mother Nature had created a ladder that enabled the cat to descend to the bottom of the bluff, but which held back man and dog. It was a tall, live-oak tree, sparsely foliaged for thirty feet up, but with plenty of branches near the top, including a large one with its longest twigs touching the rim of the bluff in places. A set of lion tracks, four in number, spaced twelve inches apart each way, showed that our elusive feline quarry had gathered herself for a leap from this spot on the rocky rim, to land on the oak limb six feet out. On observing this, I searched the top limbs and foliage with my eyes, in case our quarry had decided to hide there, but the tree was catless. I next scanned the tree-bark and saw claw marks as far down as I could view it from my position — half way to the bottom.

I laboriously retraced my downward course, finally reaching the tree that had provided such easy escape to my quarry. There I found her tracks, where she had sneaked away by keeping so close to the sheltering bluff that her body rubbed against the rocks in several places. Eli confirmed this, as he sniffed the body scent and looked up to see if the cat had climbed the vertical face above.

After passing this natural screen, the crafty animal, still loath to reveal herself for more than a few seconds, rushed in long leaps (twelve feet or more) from the sheltering bluff to a pine thicket eighty yards downhill. Just within this thicket she stopped suddenly, turning around to face the bluff she'd left in such a hurry. Evidence of this cautious move was set down in tracks pointed toward the bluff. Two sets made by her front paw-pads revealed her nervousness as she watched the back-track to learn if she was being followed by man and dog.

That she was reassured was indicated by tracks spaced some twenty inches apart, showing she had walked through the thicket to a well-worn deer runway below and turned westward on this. For the next mile or so, she prowled along this trail with a natural walking stride, until she came to the top of a short descent (about forty feet) into a shallow gulch. From a walking start, she made it to the bottom in three long leaps, and a like distance up the ascent on the farther side, in as many more. Had she charged at a deer, or heard our footsteps dogging hers? This question was answered by tracks made by a large buck as he leaped sideways to his left and cleared a growth of deer brush five feet high, just in time to escape the cat's clutch as she grappled at him and landed half a jump straight ahead in her course. Her next leap landed her right in an opening which the buck turned toward to escape. A smaller deer would have been trapped by the surrounding jungle and struck down by the cat's next rush. But the desperate buck turned as the cat rushed, and with a long leap, tried to clear the lowest hurdle — the inter-locking, topmost branches of two stiff-limbed bushes six feet high. Several tufts of hair from both animals were scattered on the ground and among the twigs and foliage. I expected to find a dead deer beyond this barrier, but found instead marks made by the buck's front hoofs as he pawed at the snow in frantic efforts to grip the ground to pull himself free. Apparently the leaping buck had fallen a couple of feet short of clearing the hedge; consequently, his hind hoofs became entangled between the cross-lacing branches and held him prisoner for a few moments. Meanwhile the bloodthirsty cat landed close behind her quarry and gripped his hips. But her hind legs also slipped through between the hedgelike branches farther back and held her there long enough for the buck — twice her weight — to kick free from both brush and claws, and make his getaway. Flecks of blood sprinkled on both sides of the buck's course at every jump he made for a couple of hundred feet told of claw marks, both right and left.

That the disappointed cat had realized defeat was plainly expressed in her own tracks spaced at a walking stride along those made by the running deer, to a point where the latter had turned downhill away from the runway both had fol-lowed until the panther rushed to attack. After losing out on this, her third chance for the day, the feline hunter turned to the runway again and followed it westerly to a point a quarter of a mile to the south of the place we had first struck her tracks this morning. Evidently we had gained on our quarry, for now her tracks were reeking with scent so fresh that Eli, by looks and actions, begged to be let loose to hunt down the exciting quarry. But I held him back, intending to wait until our quarry herself gave evidence that she knew we were gaining on her. This would be revealed by her tracks spaced either at a trotting stride, thirty inches apart, or at a loping space of twelve feet or more.

As I trailed along, with Eli in the lead and straining at his leash, I kept wondering why this hunting panther had not at any time or place during the nearly seven hours and about as many miles we had been on her trail, climbed a tree to lie in wait until some wandering deer happened to pass obligingly beneath, so that she could drop on its back. Apparently, it was not natural for her to conform to theories conceived in the imagination of our pioneers, accepted by naturalists generally, and passed down by word of mouth and in writing through succeeding generations. The way our quarry was heading, she would soon cross my tracks somewhere near the place we had passed by a half an hour before we first found her tracks this morning. Would she turn to my tracks and follow them, and so confirm stories told to me by several people who claimed that lions had followed them for several miles at different times? She did not; but crossed my plain tracks in the snow without missing a step or turning right or left. Evidently the odor of mankind failed to inspire either fear or curiosity in her feline brain, so long as the man was not in sight, or the human odor not fairly fresh. Thus, she had violated two legends this day, by running true to form. And I, a mountaineer, was learning about panthers from her. In fact, I had learned more about the habits of the American lion this day than during all my previous hunting experiences, while hunting game birds and animals native to this same region.

Continuing on the lion trail, we passed through a small thicket composed of pine, cedar and fir saplings. Here Eli stopped, sniffed to his right and tried to pull me that way. But the line of cat tracks extended ahead, so I pulled him back and pointed to the trail. Some thirty yards farther ahead the tracks ended abruptly. What had happened? I hadn't noticed any lion tracks to indicate that our quarry had turned off to either side. I looked backward along our course, but still did not see anything to solve the riddle. Then the thought struck me that Eli had already solved it ahead of time when he tried his best to turn right in the thicket. We would soon find out. I returned to the thicket and checked around its eastern edge. Eli was right. The crafty cat had emerged from that side. If she had turned that way at any place where her tracks could be plainly seen, I would have thought that she had suddenly changed her mind or else missed her goal for a short distance. However, the tactics she resorted to were apparently designed to bewilder any possible enemy, such as us, who were now closing in to bring her to bay. A close examination revealed that the hunted animal had turned halfway around and retraced her course, step for step, as marked by her own tracks in the snow.

By a further winding course of some three hundred yards, she came to the southwestern edge of a jungle composed of fir, pine and cedar saplings, averaging some twenty feet tall and carpeted underneath with snow-brush (Ceanothus cordulatus).

Here a smaller lion had come out and joined the female when she came close to the covert, then followed her back to where he had come from. Eli sniffed the air with eagerness and excitement. We had trailed our quarry to her hideout and now two of them, worthy forty dollars in bounty and thirty dollars in hides, seventy dollars in all, were silently lurking in this jungle, covering less than an acre.

But maybe they had sneaked out by the other side as we approached this one. It would be a waste of time to mess around in this snow-laden jungle if our double quarry had already escaped from the farther side. I began to circle it, while Eli kept tugging at his rope with nose ever pointing toward the inner jungle as we continued around. In spite of the dog's assurance the cats were there, I kept watching for tracks in the snow, or two tawny bodies slinking through the outer jungle. On the farther — eastern — side I did find lion tracks, two sets of them close together, but both sets were made by the paws of the young lion and pointed in opposite directions. For a few seconds I was confused, but soon realized that they were made by the young cat on his way to, and return from, the rocks he was crouched on when the old lady sent him home. The restless youngster had prowled in and out of the thicket at several other places from there on around to his meeting with his mother when she returned a few minutes ahead of us.

After making sure the cats had not given us the slip, I unleashed the dog and urged in a low voice: "Go get them, Eli." Into the thicket he went on the run, while I scrambled on top of a rock to look and listen. Within ten seconds' time, Eli began barking furiously. By this time I knew by Eli's tone the cats were standing at bay and the dog needed help. Rushing to the root end of a five-foot-thick, dead sugarpine bole lying lengthwise through the jungle, I climbed onto it and began making my way along its slippery surface, which was spotted with lion tracks pointing both ways. During the day, young Tom had promenaded forth and back for its full length of one hundred fifty feet or so.

Eli was barking "bayed" ten feet from the log near a point where it had broken by falling across a rock which held that end of the root section three feet above the ground. Apparently the cats were entrenched beneath it. When I was twenty-five feet from the break, I stopped and waited with gun ready, in case one or both of them moved out from one side or the other; but not a glimpse did I get. To my right the saplings, fifteen feet high, stood close to the log for half its length. But on the other side, there was a small opening between the cat's covert and Eli's position. I might get a shot by sliding off the log on that side while our quarry had their eyes on the dog. I tried it, but, as my feet touched the ground, Eli rushed to the break in the log, disappeared through it and raced through the jungle on a semi-circular course, yelping each second until he came around to the rock on which I had taken my first stand. Meanwhile I crept under the log where the lions had crouched at bay and found a bed of dry pine needles sheltered by the five-foot tree trunk above. The remains of a doe with ham bones stripped clean lay just beyond. Both cats had gone hunting with meat still on hand. Then Eli began barking "bayed" again. I backed out and fought through the wet jungle to its edge nearest to the dog. The young panther stood on the very rock I'd climbed when

Eli entered the thicket. His back was humped up and tail fuzzed out as he sidled about, spitting and slapping at the dog, who kept baying fiercely and leaping frantically in an effort to get his teeth into the cat's anatomy. Here was fifty pounds of cat worth fifty cents a pound to me and less than fifty feet away. Resting the carbine on the wrist of my crippled hand, I took deliberate aim and then saw that I would have to time my shooting so that the bullet would pass through the lion's chest at an instant when the dog was out of the line of fire. During the ten seconds or so spent waiting for the right moment, I began to worry about where the mother cat was, and what she would do if she saw her offspring being threatened by the courageous, wildly barking, viciously attacking dog. Was she rushing to the rescue at that moment? I pressed the trigger. The stricken cat sprang into the air, went limp and dropped sprawling behind the boulder.

I ran around the barrier, working the reloading lever as best I could while holding the barrel in the crook of my left arm. Eli was mauling the gasping kitten. The mother panther came charging toward him with tail held high and ears flattened down. We both tried to stop, as I took hasty aim and pressed the trigger. The hammer snapped on an empty chamber as the furious, snarling panther skidded almost to my feet. My arm grip hadn't held the gun muzzle from rising with the strain necessary to inject a new cartridge after the empty one was ejected. Eli was so busy mauling the kitten with all his might he didn't know what was going on, or how close he had been to death by the cat's weapons. At the gun's point, the wild creature's inherent fear of mankind overcame her anger. With marvelous speed she turned and raced toward her former covert. Meanwhile I worked the loading lever to its limit, and raised the carbine in time to take a snap-shot as the fleeing cat was nearing the thicket. She twisted, staggered, recovered and turned to the left, away from the cover she had almost gained. She must have thought the blow came from that direction.

The gun's report gave Eli his first inkling that the hunting was not over; he turned around in time to catch a glimpse of the running panther before she disappeared into another thicket to our left. After her he went, at top speed, while I followed as fast as I could. Some two hundred yards farther down, I spotted Eli racing around under a large black-oak. The wounded panther was standing in a fork twenty feet above the ground. Her tail was toward me, a small target from where I stood fifty yards from her. A bullet could enter her vital organs from this end, if it struck just right. I tried a shot. The cat pitched out and fell head-first into the snow; then began dragging her paralyzed hips toward a large cedar twenty feet away. I ran to finish her with another bullet, but Eli beat me to her, rushed in and tried for a grip on her throat. He found out this was no dying kitten, for the cat rolled over on her back, gripped him between her powerful, five-clawed (including the thumb claw) forepaws and pulled his head toward her wide-open mouth with its bone-crunching teeth. Eli struggled to escape, but the cat's claws held fast. The dog was helpless in the grasp of this natural-born killer, even when she was down and paralyzed from her shoulders backward.

To shoot at her weaving head would be to risk hitting Eli, or blasting his eardrum by the concussion. There was only one way to save him. I shoved the carbine's muzzle deep into the cat's open mouth and forced it down her throat. That did it. She released the dog and swung viciously with her left paw at my knee as I pressed the trigger. Game to the end, she had drawn blood from both enemies with a dying effort. The day's work was done, and I had a forty-dollar lien on the State of California, and probably twenty-five dollars for the hides at a private sale.

The sun was setting in a blaze of colors. The air was getting chilly. My clothing was soaked with melted snow, but I was jubilant inside. To skin the two animals would take me two hours while kneeling in the snow. My crippled left hand was numb already. My wife and kids were waiting anxiously at home, not knowing whether I would get the lions or they would get me. I decided the dead cats could keep their hides on until tomorrow. Then I could take my time and do a good job of skinning.

I headed for home with the blood-splotched Eli trotting beside me. The game dog held his head high as he trotted along, ignoring the fresh deer tracks. For the first time, he'd found game more to his liking — game that provided more sport and danger. If nothing happened to deprive me of my canine helper, our winter income was assured for as long as the cats could hold their own through propagation. If and when they become scarce in Mariposa County, I would try to persuade the Fish and Game Commission to pay me a salary and expenses to keep the lion population down in all the state game refuges. Then I would have to purchase a hound, one that bayed on the trail, and train him with Eli so I could follow the chase by sound when in strange country.

By training young dogs to carry on when the elder ones were played out, I could keep up the work until my own body gave out. These were my thoughts, as I hiked homeward with a new asset to depend on; one which would never fail me so long as I could do my part, for, unlike humans, few dogs ever fail their man in a pinch, and none because of greed or jealousy.

Killing Cougars for Bounty

The success of that first lion hunt increased my confidence of eking out a living for us that winter. Eli had proved his mettle — all I wanted now was another fall of snow to track in. This came during the evening of December 14th, and ended about 8:00 P.M., after an inch of snow had fallen. An hour later the stars were shining brightly as I went outside to check on my prospects for trailing lions the next day. Crunching of the snow underfoot indicated that a crust had already begun to form. I had hoped for a covering of six

inches, at the least — enough to last for two or three days—
and thus was not any too optimistic over the prospects when
I started out on the hunt at daybreak on the morning
of the 15th. At the last minute I decided to take Eli's brother,
Brute, along, partly to fulfill my promise to Jackson and partly
as a protection to Eli, in case we happened to have another
mixup such as menaced the life of the game hound on our
first lion hunt. Actually, Brute's presence complicated a dangerous situation later in the day.

As we left home, I noticed that the sole prints of my own
tracks made in the snow the evening before were iced over
by the freezing of moisture oozing out of the ground. This
observation, seemingly unimportant, actually provided a clue
during the early part of that day's hunt. I chose to hunt the
northern slope south of the Merced River, a choice made
for the reason that the light covering of snow would lie longer
there than on the sun-exposed southern slope across the
canyon. After wading knee-deep through the icy waters of
the river, I traveled along an old Indian trail along the stream-
bank for some two miles to the western end of a series of
granite bluffs which formed the southern wall of a gorge five
hundred feet deep and two miles long. To get past this gorge
the original makers of the trail's course — probably deer and
other species of wild animals — had turned away from the
river and traveled up a spur ridge for a half-mile to a bench-
like topography lying between the canyon rim and the steep
northern side of Wawona Point and Mt. Raymond.

When about halfway between the river and the bench, I
came across tracks made by a large coyote on the run, headed
for the river. Studying the tracks while proceeding for a hundred yards or so, I came to the place where the coyote had
come onto the trail from the southern or uphill side. The
wild canine was not chasing a deer or any other possible prey;
if he had tracks of any such quarry would be visible along
the same general course. Then why was this habitual dog-
trotter stretching itself to the limit, eight feet with each gal-
loping leap? The condition of the tracks indicated this coyote

had passed here before midnight. Suddenly I sensed that fright was the cause of the animal's actions. I could think of only two creatures who would throw such a scare into this canine predator: man or mountain lion. Since the first possibility was out of the question, it must have been a lion.

Hastily I started to back-track the coyote, hoping that here was a clue which would soon lead me to the tracks of the lion, or better still, a lion's kill — deer carcass! I couldn't afford to waste time while the light snow melted away. Not fully believing that I could have struck a clue to a nearby lion so easily, I kept searching in my mind for some other plausible explanation for the coyote's hurry. By the time we had covered some two hundred yards over a diagonal course upward along the mountainside, I conceived of another possible reason for the canine hunter's hurry, one which seemed to be more likely than my former assumption. Maybe the wild dog had heard another member of his tribe yelping for help on the trail of a deer and, dog-like, had run at full speed to get in on the chase, the kill, and the feast to follow.

While any full-grown coyote can catch and kill any deer smaller than a yearling, it takes two full-grown coyotes to bring down any adult doe or yearling buck, except when the deer is caught in snow three feet deep or more and having a crust thick enough to hold up the lighter coyote while the deer, three or four times as heavy, sinks down up to his belly. From experience, the coyote knows this and yelps for help when he thinks he needs it. This was more likely to be the explanation for the coyote's actions. He was hurrying to join in a deer chase. I must be going lion-crazy, I thought, as I turned away from the coyote tracks, and toward the path I had left.

I should have stuck by my first hunch and saved some time and energy. A quarter of a mile farther on we found cat-tracks, huge ones too, more than four inches wide and about the same length. These were half again larger than those made by the she lion I had bagged on December 3rd. I concluded they must have been made by the paws of a male lion. At first glimpse of the tracks, I judged that the cougar had prowled along here at about the time when I checked conditions in our yard — nine o'clock last evening, because the solepad prints were iced over to about the same thickness as were mine that morning. I led Brute on a rope to prevent him from chasing deer, but Eli was running loose. Sniffing the scent at once, he began checking one way and the other to determine which way the cat had headed. I helped him get started right. Then away he went on a fast dog-trot where the tracks were plain, or loping in his eagerness to find the scent in places where the prowler had changed his course. Brute sensed the excitement in the manner of both his brother and myself, and kept sniffing the tracks behind Eli.

If only the big cat had killed a deer within a couple of miles and bedded down nearby, we would surely cash in on the bounty and hide to the sum of $35.00. The way this cat was heading he would cross the tracks of the coyote within three hundred yards. Two hundred yards farther on, our quarry had stopped and crouched on his belly in the snow. From here, he had seen fit to increase his normal walking stride — two feet — to a trotting stride of three feet or so, keeping that trot uphill for a hundred feet to the base of a four-foot-thick sugar pine tree. This was getting doubly interesting, and exciting too. Had our coyote anything to do with the cat's changed course of action? Tracks showed that the lion had moved to the left or down-hill side of the tree trunk far enough to peek around it. Four feet away, between the tree and a patch of deer brush, appeared the tracks of a lone deer, which had apparently been nibbling the tenderest twigs. This is a buck about 18 months old, I thought, since it was not accompanied by others. Female deer would be in groups late in October, throughout the mating season (mid-November to mid-December) and until June 1st — close to fawning time.

Looking backward to where the lion began to trot from a crouching position, I noticed that the tree provided a screen between the feline hunter and his quarry as the latter moved toward a larger patch of deer-brush. A thickly foliaged bush close by cut off my view ahead; I moved around the tree trunk to the upper edge. Tracks showed the panther had done this before me. While I was studying the lion tracks Eli disappeared. Now I stepped out from behind the tree and saw the dog sniffing a pile of guts and bloodstains on the snow fifty feet beyond me. Tracks showed that the lion had rushed from the tree, covering the fifty feet in four leaps and struck down the deer as it stood nibbling the twigs of a bush. So swiftly and silently did the cat charge that the deer had no warning of its fate. The scene of the killing was surrounded by tracks of the killer, indicating he had been loath to leave the scene. When he did go, he took all the meat with him. Only the blood and guts, minus the liver, remained. We started out on one set of tracks, headed diagonally downhill, only to find out that the big cat had changed his mind after going a hundred feet or so, turned around and rushed back to his prize.

Then I found a clue which explained and connected the unusual actions of the two predators — the running coyote and the worried lion. The coyote had approached from above to within twenty-five feet of the entrails, stopped, shifted his paws twice, and turned westward on the run toward the spot I had backtracked it to an hour or so earlier. Five minutes more of backtracking the coyote then would have brought me to this scene of carnage and the lion's tracks. Sizing up the situation, I reconstructed it this way: When the lion caught the deer, the coyote happened to be prowling close enough to hear the terrified victim bleating and the blood-thirsty cat snarling. Dog-like, he began yapping at the disturbance. Then, sneaking close enough to witness the outcome, and get a snout full of the appetizing scent of hot venison, the coyote decided to hang around and watch for a chance to sit at second table, after the cat had gorged himself and gone away to bed down. But the lion got wise to the coyote's intentions, and prowled around and around the meat to guard it. Meanwhile the potential thief kept quiet, until the lion started to leave. As the cat moved away, the coyote came closer, but the panther had glanced backward and noticed the thief stealing to-

ward the venison. Studying the record set down in the snow by
the paws of both animals, I could almost see the huge cat, with
ears laid flat, tail held high and lips snarling angrily, charging at full speed toward the wary coyote. It's no wonder that
the latter took to his heels and kept going at full speed for
a half mile or more. Who wouldn't do likewise and lose his
appetite at the same time? Alone in the snow-covered wilderness I had a good laugh at the comic aspects of this incident
which revealed much of the biological relationship of these
two wild animals to each other.

There was still an unanswered question in my mind. Why
didn't the lion follow the normal routine for his species by
bedding near the kill to keep watch after gorging himself?
Well, let us go on with the hunt and learn about that. Out
of the maze of tracks surrounding the bloody scene, we finally
found the outgoing trail, which led us on a diagonal course
up-mountain. For several hundred feet there was no evidence
to show that the big cat was carrying a deer — not even a
blood-spot. Then going through a thicket we found tufts of
deer-hair and bloodstains on twigs and leaves. Next we came
to a bloody spot where the cat had dropped his burden, probably to rest his neck-muscles, which had borne the deer's dead-
weight for nearly a quarter of a mile, so far. That the strain
was beginning to tell, and that the cat was not holding his
head so high, was evidenced by marks made, on one side or
another, by the deer-legs dragging for several yards at a time,
for another quarter mile or so. The panther then executed a
still more remarkable stunt by carrying his difficult burden
for some twenty-five feet along a two-foot-thick, barkless, slippery log which spanned a rough gulch as deep as it was wide.
There were the big cat-tracks perfectly spaced in a two-inch
covering of snow. He had probably used this log bridge many
times on his regular prowls and now headed straight for it to
get shed of the pestering coyote, for no blunt-clawed canine
would dare to risk such a crossing, especially when the log
was covered with ice and snow.

Following the line of tracks with my eyes, I noticed a

mound composed of oak leaves and pine needles piled against the farther end of the log. This, I knew, was the feline method of caching remains of kills. I judged we would find this latest one under the mound and further that the killer would be bedded close by. Now to cross the barrier, rout our exciting quarry and force him to bay or tree where he could be seen and shot. Both dogs kept yelping shrilly as they viewed the exciting tracks they dared not follow. Darn it! I thought, they'll warn the lion to slink away and head for even rougher country. This spurred me on to seek a feasible crossing. Should we go up-mountain or down as the quickest way to find it? I chose the former course because water from rain and melting snow always gathers volume and speed while racing down-hill, thus gouging deeper and deeper the further it goes. The gorge should be much shallower farther up. Five hundred feet of steep climbing brought us to a place shallow enough for us to cross by sliding down and zigzagging up. Hurrying down to the kill, I uncovered it and found it was a buck, about 18 months old, spike antlers five inches long, and weighing about 90 pounds. Some five or six pounds of the tenderloins and upper end of one ham had been devoured.

While I was investigating, Brute started trailing downhill (northward) along the rim of the gulch, while Eli eagerly began trailing eastward. Checking first on Brute, I learned that he was back-tracking a smaller lion, a female, according to the size of the tracks. Calling him back I followed Eli and found tracks of both lions, male and female, showing they had gone away together. Here was a clue to the tomcat's motive in ignoring panther precedent from the time he'd partially dined on the deer's liver. Now it was evident to me that old Felis had another important matter to attend to, in addition to eating and sleeping. It was feline family-duty, which both Tom and Tabby Panther had been forced by hunger to forego for the time being while they hunted separately, thus doubling their chances of finding a deer and getting some venison. Tom had been successful and, after having a snack of hot liver, was anxious to find his mate and escort her to a midnight supper. But the coyote entered the scene just in time to interfere with the usual panther procedure. So Tom, to make sure of food for his mate carried all the meat with him while looking for her. Maybe they had arranged to meet at the log-bridge, or perhaps both had used it many times before and instinctively headed for it as the shortest way to a crossing of the difficult gulch between them. Who knows? Animals seem to have mysterious but effective means of getting messages across to each other.

Curiously enough, this was the only time I was ever to know of one lion carrying food to another one, either mate or off-spring. But then, neither did I ever again encounter the same set of circumstances during some seven thousand lion hunts, which netted nearly seven hundred members of the species dead or alive.

Trailing the two cougars for a mile or more eastward, up the river canyon, we came to the top edge of a granite cliff some thirty feet high and five hundred feet long. Leaning against this bluff, at an angle of 45 to 50 degrees, was the charred heart of a cedar tree trunk averaging 12 inches in diameter. Both panthers had used this as a ladder to descend head-first to the bottom of the cliff. I peeked over the cliff edge and saw a double line of panther-tracks extending twenty feet from the base of the cat's ladder into the entrance of a sort of cave formed by a slab of rock which leaned against the main bluff. Our quarry had to be hiding there, because the farther end of this granite-walled room was closed by other slabs. I held my carbine ready, in case either one of them showed itself. Both dogs sensed the tension and began yapping shrilly as they crowded each other to get a paw-hold on the lion's slippery ladder. Both were in danger of losing their grip and falling. Dropping my carbine behind me, I leaned forward and gripped their collars so that I could pull them back to safety. As I struggled, two tawny feline forms rushed from the den with marvelous speed. The smaller one dodged down-hill and around out of sight below the base of the slab. The larger one, who appeared to be three feet tall and ten feet long, sprang onto a log which lay alone down the steep hill. Apparently, he hadn't counted on a layer of ice beneath a two-inch covering of snow for he slid downward along the log, until his belly struck the jagged end of a dead limb. His mouth flew open and let out a loud grunt and a sickly yowl. Then sliding off the log he trotted away in the direction taken by his mate.

Both dogs had seen the big cat and went wild with excitement. With both hands full trying to keep them from dashing over the cliff in pursuit, I had no chance to get in a shot. It was like a nightmare, as I stood helpless to prevent seventy dollars worth of cat hides and bounties from slipping through my fingers, when, with a gun in my hands, I could have dropped them with one shot apiece. It was rough and dangerous country, but the dogs might be able to tree them yet. I leashed the dogs on the lead-rope and coaxed and dragged them along the rim to the nearest end, down to the bottom, where I let them go. By the time I reached the cave the dogs were yapping near the river some two hundred yards beyond and below. Leaving the cats to them for the time being, I stopped to examine the big lion's skidway and found a patch of lion hide the size of a fifty-cent piece hooked on the sharp end of the snag which the cat's belly had hit. Something else had happened to him too, for the sole-pad prints of one fore-paw was soaked with blood as far as I could view them on the course of his get-away. Examining the hide-out, I found it to be some twelve feet long and six feet wide at the floor, which was covered with dry sand. Marks made there by cat-shanks and belly revealed that this was, indeed, the feline honeymoon cottage, and a perfect one it was for that purpose.

The dogs were still yapping intermittently, but not barking "treed." I ran to help them and found they were baffled. I scanned all the trees — dozens of them — mostly live oak and fir, all abundantly foliaged. There wasn't a cat to be found. Then, peering over the edge of a ten-foot cliff I saw big, blood-stained cat-tracks imprinted in snow covering a boulder near mid-stream. The male lion, at least, had sprung off the cliff and headed across the river. Calling to the dogs I worked up-stream beyond the cliff and waded across. Coming down the northern bank I found tracks of the female, pointed in the right direction to join the male on a polished granite surface a hundred feet or so uphill from the river. The sun had beaten down on this southern exposure with the result that water was trickling fairly evenly over the hard surface. The dogs did their best to work out the diluted scent, which was an hour old by now, but it was no use. So far as trailing went we lost out at the river bank. But I could see snow on trees and ground a quarter-mile above us.

Setting myself down on a rock I thought out a plan which might save the day for us: I intended to work up-river for a quarter-mile, then leftward up-mountain for half a mile and keep to the snowline westward for half a mile and down toward the river a quarter-mile below where our quarry had crossed. If they had gone up-mountain I would see their tracks in snow. If up- or down-river the dogs may be able to get the scent from bushes or tracks on the drier rocks. But I never got a chance to carry out this plan, for, as I got to my feet, a thrill-ing sound reached my ears, a hoarse caterwaul. It sounded like a bass-voiced imitation of the familiar feline yowl commonly uttered by domestic female cats when mating. Breathlessly, I waited for a repeat. It came almost immediately from a dense thicket of cedar and pine saplings and deer brush, over which towered spreading live-oaks growing along the base of a gran-ite bluff some four hundred feet above us. Apparently, these honeymooning felines had done just what I hoped they would do in the circumstances — loiter in the first suitable cover to continue their love affair. The dogs cocked their ears and looked at each other in a knowing way. I started on the double-quick to take advantage of the situation while our unsuspecting quarry were concentrating on gratifying the mating instinct. The dogs rushed past me and raced toward the feline love-nest.

Before I could cover half the distance, they were barking "treed" with a vim. "Good boys," I yelled. I should have kept my mouth shut, for when I reached the live-oak, which both dogs were trying to climb, our panthers were gone. Thinking the dogs may be barking up the wrong tree, I scanned the branches of other trees nearby. Then I noticed that the branches of one fork of the first tree overhung the brow of the cliff some twenty-five feet above us. This was their out. We had to lose several more minutes working westward along the base to find a place to climb to the top, then the same distance back to the cat's ladder. There were the tracks, but the felines had separated. One, the female, had trotted up a gulch covered with pine saplings. The male turned eastward and kept to the rim of the bluff which had provided the escape route. His right forepaw was still bleeding enough to stain its tracks. He was the one I wanted. All day I'd been hankering to pull a bead on the huge varmint. His tracks couldn't be more than five minutes old. Both dogs took off on the run. Breathless with effort and excitement, I tried to keep near them, meanwhile keeping both ears open for the longed-for message from the dogs telling that the panther was treed. But it didn't come. What was the matter? The dogs were still somewhere ahead.

After a half-mile race I saw them circling a large, thickly foliaged cedar in a draw a hundred yards beyond and as many feet below a point I stood on. From here, I searched the tree from base to crest, without sighting our quarry. The dogs circled closer in and finally pawed the tree-bark and began telling me the game was up. I moved closer and searched again. Nothing doing. Next I circled the tree, far enough away, I thought, to scan every possible hiding place for such a large animal. Still no sight of our bewildering quarry. He must have tricked his pursuers by doubling back after pawing the tree-bark to leave misleading scent there. Sizing up the situation I noticed the cedar stood some fifteen feet above the brow of a bluff which slanted downward nearly vertical for some fifty feet. Water seeping from the draw made the granite slippery for the full length of fifty feet, or so. No animal, not even a panther, could possibly traverse the steep, slippery surface. Leaving the dogs barking by the tree, I doubled back above the dangerous rim for some two hundred feet, then turned uphill, following a continuous covering of snow, crossed our incoming tracks and continued checking loopwise until I arrived back at my starting point. No lion had left that area. Several large trees stood within the loop. I looked them over from top to bottom. But no lion was in sight. Then I got another idea: Why waste time here? We'd better go back and give the female a run. She may not be so smart. I called the dogs away against their will and began retracing our steps toward where the pair of big cats had parted company.

Halfway on the new trail, I woke up to the fact that since he couldn't fly, the big lion had to be hiding inside the loop I had traced. Then I recalled one slip I had made while looking for him. On each round I had made of the cedar, I had avoided passing through a small thicket of wet deer-brush growing between the tree and the bluff. I hurried back, with both dogs confidently running ahead, entered the thicket, looked up and saw a huge cat head with startled round eyes peering down from under a thick bunch of top foliage. As the cat's eyes caught mine, his mouth opened wide and emitted a panther-sized hiss. His husky chest offered a perfect target. Then I made a mistake by being too anxious. I should have tied each dog away from the danger zone with his own lead-rope, which I carried.

As it happened, I drew a hasty bead on the cat chest and pressed the trigger. Down he came, crashing limbs and foliage as he fell more than a hundred feet. The dogs went wild: I dodged out of the way just in time to escape being crushed by the falling body. The dogs tore into it, attacking the twisting, snarling head. His body was paralyzed from the collar-bone rearward, and thus was harmless. Having landed with his head end downhill, he kept sliding with the smoothness of the body hair.

Both dogs took their turns at gripping an ear on their respective sides of the snarling cat head, letting go as the cat

twisted to spit in each dog's face in turn. Within ten seconds
dogs and cat had slid downhill to within five feet of the jump-
off, with the frantic dogs backing toward destruction. I had
to do something quickly. There was one chance. I dropped
the gun, grabbed the cat's tail, bending it halfway around a
handy cedar sapling and held on for dear canine lives. Meanwhile I coaxed and cussed the dogs by spells to get them away
from the danger point. At any moment either one might crowd
the other over the edge to death or disablement. Desperate,
I thought of the rope in my jumper pockets. My crippled left
hand could not hold the strain. Finally, I managed to hook
a stiff numb finger in a coil of rope and pull it out. It was
fitted with a loop on one end. Reaching for the cat's hind
foot, I worked the rope around it, passed the end through the
loop, slid it above the hock joint and took up the slack. With
this to hold onto, if the tail-hold slipped, I placed both knees
on the cat's tail and quickly took two turns of the rope around
the sapling and tied it there. All this time, perhaps three
minutes (which seemed an hour), the dogs and cat kept
barking, biting, snarling and spitting with a vengeance.
Getting out my other rope I carefully worked the end through
both dogs' collars, pulled them away from the bluff and held
them out of danger. The fatally wounded cat seemed as full
of fight as when he landed on the ground with a bullet through
his chest and his spine shattered between the shoulders. I
finished him with a bullet through the brain.

Skinning the cat took an hour, for every inch of the hide,
like that of a bear, had to be cut loose from his tough flesh
and muscles. He measured seven feet, including a thirty-three-
inch tail. Five miles of fast hiking brought me home by the
time darkness fell.

*   *   *

Following the second successful lion hunt I took to the
woods with dogs and gun during and after every storm,
bagging eleven lions, two bears and an even dozen lynxcats
by April 8th, all of which brought in four hundred and forty
dollars, not counting some fifty pounds of bear lard we used

for cooking purposes. Add to this the one hundred dollars I earned making Big Trees souvenirs for Baxter and I averaged $125 per month, working about half the time. This was as much money as I had been paid for working ten hours per day for thirty days a month in the mines. Furthermore, I was becoming quite well known as a lion hunter, through accounts published in newspapers.

My luck continued to improve. One day a big car arrived and a familiar looking man got out, came up to me and asked: "Aren't you Jay Bruce?" "Yes," I said. "And you are Bob Sherman." Bob had gone fishing with me several times during the summer of 1899, while I was catching trout for the hotel, and had become a skillful angler during that time. When I first met him in 1899, Bob was vacationing at Wawona, after making a name for himself in football at the University of California. In fact he had been the outstanding player of the season. After graduating from U.C. he had entered business and made a fortune.

He asked me what my plans were. "I know of two fairly good horses which I can get by paying a twenty-dollar feed bill on them. I am going to start out with them and build up a business conducting parties on hunting and fishing trips," I replied. Then he told me he had many friends who would pay well to be taught how to catch trout enough to satisfy their own needs. "I'll send you enough customers to keep you busy the rest of this season," he offered. Thus, I was launched in a game I liked, one which from the beginning brought returns five times that of my pay from Baxter at the Big Trees.

I knew that I would need a good jump dog if I was to provide deer hunters a reasonable chance of getting a shot at the wary game; a dog which would wind a deer in its covert, chase it out and run it down after it had been shot and crippled. Would Eli take to deer hunting after trailing only lions and bears for two winters? I tried him out, at the risk of spoiling him for lion trailing. I began by pointing to buck-tracks I wanted him to follow and urging him on, until the game was jumped and shot. Among other things, he soon learned not to chase any deer more than a few hundred yards unless it was bleeding. By the end of that season Eli had developed into a perfect deer dog. I still had some misgivings as to the effect of deer hunting on his ability to track lions later on. When the time came I kept a watchful eye on him until he stopped to sniff fresh deer-tracks and then warned him, "No, no, Eli. Let him go." One such warning proved to be enough. Apparently he understood that deer hunting was over and lion hunting in order, for he took off with confidence on the first lion trail we crossed, trailed all day without making any break and treed the feline quarry at sundown. From this time on he was a lion hunter first, a bear hunter second and wildcatter third, until deer season opened again the following August 15th. Now I had a dependable canine partner in the hunting field.

After a successful season in 1917, conducting parties on expeditions after trout, deer and bear, I took my horses to pasture among the foothills for the winter, while I set out on lion and bear trails on foot. By April 27, 1918, I had added to my record five more bears, twice as many lynxcats and ten lions, four of these being taken on one day. This happened when Eli, Brute and I trailed a mother cougar to her lair, located in a sort of den among some rocks on the mountain-side within a mile and a half of our house. As the she-cat stood at bay defending her young, I had to shoot her in close quarters. Then shedding my denim jumper, I gathered the three spotted kittens into it and carried them home. Even at their tender age (approximately nine days), they exhibited all the fierceness of their tribe, clawing and biting feebly at my hands all the way.

I phoned Townsley, Chief Ranger for the Yosemite Park, and told him how and where they were captured. The next day he came to my place to get them and take them into the Valley, where they were cared for by the children of Gabriel Souveleski for some three months. The three kittens were put on exhibition with a cash box beside the cage, bringing in some $5,000 for the Red Cross fund within a few months after the Park Service took them. Meanwhile, a naturalist had ruled that they be denied any raw meat, their natural food after weaning time. As a result, two of them, a male and a female, died in convulsions. Thereafter the remaining female was given fresh meat and liver, on my recommendation, and lived out her natural life-span of fifteen years in a cage with a male cougar brought from Yellowstone Park.

That spring I started out with six horses of my own and catered to patrons of the hotel exclusively, earning five hundred dollars per month between April 1st and the closing of deer season on October 15th.

Having seen tracks of two lions only on my trips all summer, I thought it time to approach the Fish and Game Commission with a proposition to hunt lions for them all winter in game refuges where people were not allowed to hunt deer. This I did as soon as deer season closed. Bear season opened the same day. By November 1st, I had bagged three and put up our winter supply of bear lard. Just as a novelty I also cured some side meat and smoked it on the model of bacon.

On December 23, Ranger Townsley called me and told me that a group of influential people were due to arrive the next day to start a fund to promote an all-year highway up the Merced River canyon. He suggested I tell some lion stories on Christmas eve. He ended by saying significantly, "Two members of the Fish and Game Commission will be here to talk about building a state fish hatchery here. So be sure and be here, and we might start something in favor of your plan." Here at last was hoped for favorable action on my application.

Leaving home at seven o'clock in the morning, I hiked the twenty-six miles, part of the way through snow a foot deep, and arrived at Townsley's office at one o'clock in the afternoon, bringing Eli with me, as Townsley had advised. After dinner we all congregated in the hotel lounge, where Mr. Steve Mather, then Director of National Parks, started off with the account of a bear hunt he had participated in several

years before. Having set the stage and created the right atmosphere, Mr. Mather introduced me as a famous lion hunter,
whose work had been responsible for a marvelous increase
in the park deer. I told my story, one which was later used
by the famous novelist, Peter B. Kyne, as the theme for a story
entitled *Semper Fidelis.*

When I finished, the two representatives of the Fish and
Game Commission, Edward L. Bosqui and Carl Westerfeldt,
went into a huddle for a minute or so. Then they came to me,
and Ned Bosqui said: "We read your letter some time ago
and held a meeting to discuss it. But no one thought it was
practicable, because we couldn't see how you could tell where
to find lions in localities strange to you, nor how you could
keep from getting lost. But after hearing you talk tonight,
Carl and I believe you can make good so we are appointing
you now. Go to San Francisco and fix up the appointment
with Joe Hunter before January 1st." Eli, too, had made a
profound impression on the officials because of his record
of having forced thirty-one lions to tree, during three winters.
From Townsley's office I telephoned the good news to my wife.

IV

OFFICIAL COUGAR KILLER FOR
THE STATE OF CALIFORNIA

ΛΛΛΛΛΛΛΛΛΛΛΛΛΛΛΛΛΛΛΛΛΛΛΛΛΛΛΛΛΛ

Life Habits of the Cougar

THE QUESTION of how to find lions in strange country, first raised by Commissioner Ned Bosqui when he considered my appointment, was asked by Joe Hunter when confirming my appointment at the main office in San Francisco. The answer is really quite simple. Records show that the Fish and Game Commission had paid bounties on some twenty-five hundred lions, over a period of twelve years, beginning on November 1, 1907 and up to January 1, 1919, when my appointment was to take effect. Every one of those claims for bounty were made on an official form, which had to be notarized. Among other information, they contained a description of the locality where that particular lion was taken, and the name and address of three witnesses who had seen the fresh hide shortly after said animal was taken. Then each lion hide had to be sent to the main office to be marked "canceled." Referring to the information contained in the claims for bounty, I told Joe Hunter: "I can sit here in your office and go over five hundred or so of those claims and learn where each one of those lions was taken in different parts of the state. I will thus learn all the lion country that way if necessary." I further remarked that I was counting on the probability that reports of lion damage would be coming in thick and fast from all lion country in the state, as soon as newspaper publicity reached those outlying areas. As to that, the news of my appointment had already been published in every part in the state.

Joe Hunter then reached into his drawer, brought out a letter, and said: "Here is one that came in yesterday from our Deputy in Tulare County, reporting that a lion killed eight goats in one night a month or so ago, at Camp Nelson, and requesting that you be sent there at once. Go to Porterville, and contact Oliver Brownlow; he will take his horse and pack in your equipment."

So it was that I started on my first official lion hunt with only one trained dog, Eli. But for effect I took along an aristocratic airedale, named Mike, which Townsley had wangled from some breeder and given me. As a lion hunter, Mike proved to be a total loss. Not having any car at the time, I had to travel by train to Springville, and hike sixteen miles from there, while the game warden, Oliver Brownlow, rode horseback. That first night we stayed in his summer cabin.

The next morning I started hunting and trailed a female lion until noon, on tracks two days old, lost the trail where deer had over-run the lion tracks, then came to camp and had lunch. There I found Brownlow lying sick in bed with a cold. After resting for an hour and studying a map of the area, I said to Brownlow: "I think I know where that cat is right now, so I'm going out again and ought to have her before night." Two hours later, I walked in carrying a 90-pound, pregnant cougar draped around my neck. During the next two weeks I bagged two more lions, another female and a male. Five lynx also fell victim to me and my dog.

After paying a visit home, I was sent to Tuolumne County, where a ditch tender had reported seeing tracks of four lions traveling together. Thinking I might need a horse to use in packing supplies and equipment, I walked down to Elkhorn Ranch and got one of my horses and saddles and rode by way of Coulterville to Buck Meadow, a station on the Big Oak Flat Road to Yosemite. With the dogs following close behind, I made the trip of some fifty miles in two days.

Snow was falling next morning when I walked three miles

to the ditch camp, and met Jim Scofield, the ditch tender who hàd reported seeing the tracks of four lions. Since he had to patrol the ditch for six miles to its intake, he went with me now. On the way he pointed out the place where the four lions had crossed the ditch, going north toward Hardin Ridge across the canyon of the South Fork of the Tuolumne River. The snow had been falling since dawn, covering all tracks made before that time. This would be no more than a scouting trip for me, I thought. But one never can tell what will happen for sure on any lion hunt. After reaching the intake of the ditch, I decided to continue the hunt by returning along the backbone of Hardin Ridge, on the chance that some hungry or restless cougar might go prowling by daylight on such a stormy day.

As we plodded along, up-hill and down, through snow-laden thickets of ceanothus and mahogany, and forests of pine, cedar and oak, the snow kept piling deeper and deeper, until by late afternoon it was knee-deep when we came to the western point of Hardin Ridge. Suddenly Eli, who was ahead of us, started to bark excitedly.

We ran down through the snow-laden jungle with Mike keeping close to our heels until we almost stumbled over the half-devoured remains of a big doe, surrounded by tracks of half-grown lions. Fifty yards beyond stood Eli on his hindlegs with both forepaws braced against the trunk of a small oak tree, while he barked furiously up at two half-grown cougars growling down from snow-packed branches one cougar-jump above him. Two quick shots from my carbine brought them down dead. Where was Mike, a member of a breed that was expected to do everything any other dog would do and then lick the other dog? Well, he was calmly dining on venison reeking with cougar scent.

Mad as a wet hen and too anxious to get after the remaining member of this trio of young cats, I pulled a boner and got Eli started off on the outgoing tracks of the mother cougar, who had gone on a hunt from here some three hours earlier, I judged from the fact that her tracks were half-filled with snow. The faithful dog took after their maker, and there was no stopping him. I knew he would pursue this cougar until he either treed or lost out because of something destroying her tracks and scent. Perhaps Mike would do his part for once. Seizing his collar, I dragged him away from the deer carcass and led him until we came to the fresh tracks made by the remaining young cat who had dashed away when Eli surprised the trio. Mike wouldn't even look at the tracks. I shoved his fool nose down into the reeking paw-prints and urged him to go after the varmint. It was no use. He refused to be coaxed or brow-beaten into taking any part in the hunting. We started to skin the two dead cougars while waiting and hoping for Eli to return.

Twenty minutes later we started down toward the river, each one of us carrying a lion hide with the skull and paws still unskinned, for skinning them would have taken too much time. As it was, we would have to move fast in order to reach camp before darkness overtook us. Ten minutes of walking took us half-way down to the river, and Eli had failed to overtake us so far. But Mike still kept close to our heels. Then a familiar sound caught my ears; Eli's voice barking "treed" somewhere within a couple of hundred yards. But because of roaring of the stream below us and an echo rebounding from the farther canyon-side, we could not tell from what direction the dog's voice was coming. Ten to one Eli had started to follow our tracks and caught scent of the remaining young lion and taken after and treed it. Then he would be to our right, since we had not crossed the tracks on our way down. We turned that way and soon located the dog. Five minutes later we had another cat in the bag, or ready to be skinned. However, we did not stop for that; instead I shouldered our latest victim and carried it to camp, while Jim carried both hides. The next day I learned that Eli had trailed the mother lion for more than a mile and then lost track of his quarry, where a band of deer had tramped over the lion tracks and overcome their scent. During the next three nights the mother cougar spent most of the time searching for her lost offspring. This I learned by going back and trailing her for several hours each day.

The first day we struck tracks of another and younger female, trailed her to a fresh kill and bagged her. The second day an oversized male cougar crossed the trail of the mother cat, after the latter had passed there. Switching to the fresher tracks, Eli trailed five miles and treed the big cat, which I killed. With nothing to interfere, we bagged the mother cougar on the third day after bagging her offspring. Although she had prowled for several hours each night around the place where her kittens had been left by her and killed by me, and although this place was within hearing range of our camp, we failed to hear any sounds to indicate that she called loudly to her lost young ones. I have no doubt but that she did call many times, but it would be a bird-like call, resembling that uttered by a red-tailed hawk, but less raucous, if anything.

Thus I bagged six lions during the first four days of hunting in a locality utterly strange to me.

It was during this year that Eli came down with a case of distemper and, being feverish, sought every cold spring to cool himself in. As a result of this the distemper developed into pneumonia. I had to get him to a veterinarian. Packing him on my back, in a knapsack, I walked twelve miles to Buck Meadow, where I then proceeded by auto to Berkeley, where my family had moved the previous May. A month later Eli was able to be up and go hunting, but his vocal cords, like those of Pike of the rattlesnake episode, had become so affected that his voice was only a hoarse whisper. Because of losing that month while Eli was layed up and being hampered by his partial disability for the next two months my catch of lions that first year of my service with the Fish and Game Commission, was only twenty-six lions — six less than I had expected to bag. One of these, a female, hunting to feed one young one, had killed eight goats during one month. Another one, an adult male, had killed three hundred goats at the Ralph Ranch during one year. Still another one, a half-grown male, had started killing goats and done away with six within one month before I arrived to end his career of slaughter.

By the end of 1921, I had covered enough of the lion country of California to be able to plot the life-zone of the cougars in all of the Sierra Nevadas and that part of the Cascade Range extending into California. I found that lion country lay between three thousand and five thousand feet elevation. Looking for maps one day, I found one which showed the various zones of temperature indicated by different colors. Comparing this with the lion belt I had traced on a map of California, I discovered that the belt shown in green coincided exactly with the lion belt in the Sierra Nevada and those sections of the northern Coast Range where I had found cougars. I assumed that, since cougars usually ran true to form, all the parts of the state shown in green on the map, being of like temperature, would be inhabited by cougars. Counting the number of townships marked in green on my map, I found there were six hundred of them, or 21,000 square miles of lion country in California.

While I was discussing this with Joe Hunter for the first time, he brought out a large map of the state and asked me to trace lines around the lion country as I had found it. After this was done he had a number of his office force go over some five hundred claims for bounty and stick a pin in the map at each place where lions had been taken. The result confirmed my own experience. Ninety-nine percent of those five hundred cougars had been taken in the area enclosed in my lines. This was true in Southern California as well as the central and northern mountains. From this time on my findings were generally accepted. With the life-zone of the cougar determined, it was an easy matter for me to estimate the cougar population of California. For instance, I had found the density of population to be one cougar to the township. This doesn't mean that each lion lives within one township. Usually, there are four cougars, say, ranging over that many townships. The average works out to one per township. By counting the number of townships included in the green temperature belt, we found there were a total of six hundred townships. Allowing one cougar for each township, we estimated there should be six hundred lions in the state. In fact this estimate has been confirmed by everything we have learned about the cougar life-history during the last thirty years. In addition to (or as a result of) proper elevation, temperature, cover, and vegetation, good lion country maintains four deer, at least, to each square mile. Eighty square miles of such mountain area could support an average-sized panther family consisting of Tom, Tabby and two kittens per year, and still maintain a breeding stock of 100 female deer of breeding age (18 months and older), 100 potential breeders coming on to replace those lost by natural causes, and 120 male deer. Judging from my observations made during some fifty years spent in the wilds, I would say that the natural reproduction in the deer family averages one and one-half fawns per doe per year (one to three in a litter). At this rate our 100 breeding females would bring forth 150 fawns. Now anyone might wonder what becomes of those 150 deer born each year, what prevents them from over-stocking the mountain ranges within a few years. Well, one family of cougars will account for 100 of them, including some of all ages, from newly born fawns to old timers tottering on their last legs. Human hunters with guns probably bring down 15 — all of them bucks — leaving 35, mixed in sizes and sex, to fall prey to coyotes, wildcats, foxes and bears. With all these living menaces to deer life, and loss caused by starvation at times when deer become stalled in deep snow at places over-grazed by range cattle in summer, it is unlikely that any more than ten percent of the deer born ever live out their reproductive period in life, let alone their natural life-span of fifteen years.

*   *   *

The next few years were adventuresome, interesting and profitable. By 1927, I had six thoroughly trained hounds to depend on. In that year, I was able to make my biggest catch, taking forty-three cougars, including three half-grown ones and two smaller ones, which I took alive and sold to zoos.

1928 started off just as successfully. For one thing, I had along my eldest son, Jay Jr., fifteen years old, whose job it was to operate a motion picture camera, with the idea of finishing a movie of lion hunting, one that I had been working on since 1925. The twenty-seventh of June came as any other day. Then something happened I had been half expecting and fearing ever since I started hunting lions, something which had nearly happened many times.

We were chasing a big male cougar through dense thickets of hazel and manzanita with three dogs, Ranger, Bruce, and Pete, worrying the quarry around and around us in this jungle, when my left eye was roughly jabbed by a sharp-ended stalk. The shock was so severe that I fell backward in a sitting position. Just then the dogs began barking "treed" several hundred feet down the Rubicon River slope. My son, seeing what had occurred, took my hand and led me stumbling over rough ground to where the dogs were barking around a big cedar tree. By now I could catch glimpses of the cougar standing on a limb fifty feet above the ground. If the boy made a bad shot it might cost the life of a dog, so I insisted that he put leashes on them so I could hold them from rushing into battle with the cougar if the latter fell out wounded too badly to get to and climb another tree. While I held the three dogs Jay Jr. took aim and fired. The cat sprang into space, came down, sprang to his feet and took off downhill with a young hound, Duke II, baying madly in pursuit for some two hundred yards. Then suddenly he ceased baying. Telling the boy to run down there in case the cat was wounded and down, I followed slowly, trying to watch my step between fluttering eyelids, as the frantic dogs tugged violently and thrashed around at the end of their leashes, trying to get free. Soon the boy yelled, saying that the lion was up a big fir tree. "Don't shoot until I get there," I ordered.

By this time I could hold my uninjured right eye open long enough to take aim. I took the revolver and handed the leashes over to my son. The big cougar looked sick, with blood oozing out from a bullet wound through the middle of his body. Standing directly beneath him I took aim up at a spot between his forelegs, and pressed the trigger. Down he came again, sprang to his feet and took off like a streak downhill toward the Rubicon River a half-mile below. Now we let go of Pete, the silent trailer, successor to Eli. A few minutes later he began barking "treed" close to the river. Somehow, I got down there and finished the lion with a bullet through the heart.

While skinning him we found that my first bullet had struck a little to one side and passed upward between the cat's shoulder and chest. Skinning that cat, even with the aid of my son was an endless job. After it was done, the boy took the hide and started ahead, while I took my time climbing a mile up the steep river hill. On reaching the rim I found the hide hanging on an oak limb at the end of a road where Jay Jr. was to meet me with the car. There I sat for nearly two hours while the boy walked five miles to where the car had been left when we found the lion tracks at daybreak this morning, got the car and drove it back to me.

We were camped near Uncle Tom's Cabin, a stopping place on one of the immigrant roads crossing the Sierra Nevada Summit. At once the proprietress, Mrs. Archie (Irma) Lawyer, kindly gave up her room and bed to me. I spent the next three days lying in a darkened room with boric acid solution dripping on a pad covering the torn cornea of my left eye. Although I was convinced from the first that the vision was totally destroyed, I did not want to go home before making sure. Thus, it was three days later that I reached San Francisco and was sent to a hospital under the provision of the State Compensation Act.

After lying for three weeks in a hospital bed, with both eyes bandaged between treatments, I was allowed to go home. However, I was not allowed to go hunting again until October 1st. From that day on, for the next twenty years, I knew that I would be taking the risk of suffering a miserable, lingering death every time I went hunting alone, and this was most of the time, since nearly all my lion hunting was done by myself and in lonely, rugged areas.

Truly Man's Best Friends

At this point you might be interested in a history of my dogs. You already know about Eli and Ranger. Scout was the offspring of Ranger and a female hound I purchased from a mid-western kennel in 1919. Although she herself was too delicate to stand the strain of cougar hunting, she had good blood lines. A year later (1920) Scout's dam was again bred to Ranger and in due time brought forth a litter of eight pups. One of these, a male, was purchased by Wm. Sanborn Young, who later was elected to the California State Senate, for several terms, and then became a member of the Geneva Conference on narcotics. Senator Young named the pup Bruce, after me, kept him for a year, and then decided Bruce should be following in his dad's footsteps, instead of making life miserable for two bird dogs belonging to the Senator. Thus Bruce became part of my lion hunting pack. In 1925, I retired Eli at the ripe old age of eleven. Duke had been killed shortly before, when he plunged over a 300-foot bluff as he chased a cougar.

Starting in 1923, I did some experimental breeding, trying to embody the special qualifications of Eli, Ranger and Duke into one special strain of hunting dog which would follow a cold trail silently, make a fast finish, tree lions and keep them treed for ten or twelve hours at a time, barking constantly during all that time. One of the resulting pups brought forth in 1924, after three cross-breedings, was a female, whom I named Diana, after the mythical goddess of the chase. I presented her to a special friend and companion of several lion hunts, Tommy Stephenson, of Hollister, California. Two others, both male, I kept for a year, getting them well started in lion hunting. Then I got a letter from the Canadian Government inquiring if I had a couple of trained lion dogs to sell.

After some correspondence, I sold the two young dogs, shipping them to Vancouver, B. C., where they made a record as cougar hunters during the following two years, after which both were killed, one by a cougar and the other by the kick of a horse. This I learned when the same official wrote me again to purchase two more dogs of the same strain. Meanwhile, one of the links in that chain of breeding had died from picking up poison bait put out for coyotes. Her only living descendant was Diana. So far, the only personal experience I'd had regarding the hunting ability of members of my special strain of lion dog was what I had seen those two pups do before they were a year old and had been sold to the Canadian Government.

It was Pete's untimely death (he was killed by a cougar) that brought an opportunity for me to really try out the only living member of that litter I had so carefully bred. On hearing of Pete's tragic death, Tommy Stephenson proved to be a friend in need by offering to give Diana back to me. She had proven to be a silent trailer when hunting lynx around Hollister, and Tommy knew I would need one, now that Pete was gone. Returning from Los Angeles County, about June 1st, I went to my old stamping ground at Wawona and, on the first day of hunting there, trailed a mother cougar and her three kittens, two male and one female, about six weeks of age.

The first one treed was a male kitten which I captured within a mile of our homestead house, and put in a suitable cage there, later giving it to the Yosemite zoo.

Going back the next day I struck the tracks of the daddy cougar and trailed him for ten miles to the crest of the Chowchilla Mountain. I then gave up the trail, intending to hunt down the other three — mother, brother and sister of my captured kitten — while waiting for the big tomcat to make his round and come back to this area.

That evening I received a telephone message, saying that a big lion had killed 16 sheep in Round-tree Saddle the night before. Starting early I reached the scene by six o'clock and found that the killer had returned and dragged one of his victims away. Following this trail for some five hundred feet toward Devil's Gulch, the dogs jumped him from a kill and treed him close by. I knew this to be the same cougar I had trailed the day before, for his tracks were headed down a trail leading to this cove and no more than three miles from where I turned back. Tracks showed that he had come to this place by this same trail. I made sure that Diana was present at the capture and killing and knew at once that she was a natural-born lion hunter. She was proving to be the exact type of cougar hunter I had in mind when I began the experimental breeding. Consequently I bred her to Bruce and carried on the strain for three more generations, every individual of which proved to be a natural cougar hunter.

After bagging the mother cougar and the litter brother to the captured one, I drove up to Arnold's Lodge, a stopping place on the road to Calaveras Grove of Big Trees, to investigate a report of lion tracks seen near there. Arriving in a snowstorm, late in the afternoon, I stayed there overnight. It happened that I had with me the tanned hide of a large male lion. Mrs. Arnold wanted to buy the hide but was undecided as to whether she ought to spend the money.

Meanwhile, I had noticed a bob-tailed, husky dog, which appeared to be a mixture of airedale and German police dog. The only thing I disliked about him was his name, Mike, but I could change that without confusing in any way the dog. I offered to trade my lion hide for the dog. The result was, I took Mike with me and she kept the lion hide. Once out of hearing of his former owner, Mike became Spike and responded to the change without noticing it.

From Arnold's, I went to Hospital Rock in Sequoia National Park and bagged nine lions during January, February and March. Two of these, a fifty-pound male and a thirty-pound female, we captured alive, and were raised by a friend of mine, Earl Moncrief, father of Charlie Moncrief, who pitched in the big league for several seasons. Earl, who was a sportsman at heart and hunter by nature, helped in the capture of these as well as several others he kept at his place of business in Parlier, Fresno County.

Spike, after once tasting cougar blood, never let any other dog get ahead of him on a lion trail, treeing approximately a hundred and fifty cougars during the next seven years. In January 1931, shortly after Spike had proved his mettle, I retired Ranger, who was nearing fourteen years. I left Ranger with Earl Moncrief, who offered to give him a home in his barn. A few days later he slipped his collar, got out to a highway at night and was struck and killed by a speeding automobile. So ended the career of a marvelous cougar hunter.

DEATH OF RANGER EVOKES SYMPATHY OF HUMAN FRIENDS

It is not often that a dog rates a resolution of respect, even though many deserve them. But when Ranger, one of the stars of the pack of J. Bruce, official lion hunter of California and a friend of many Tulare sportsmen, died in Three Rivers these sportsmen felt that some official observance of his demise should be made.

For this reason the officers of the local fish and game association passed the following resolution:

IN MEMORIAM: Whereas, in His infinite wisdom the Great Father of Nature, who controls all animal destinies, has seen fit to remove from our midst Ranger, a true friend and pal, whose passing to the happy hunting grounds of His Father leaves us with a great sense of our great loss, and

Whereas, during his long and useful life he endeared himself to those with whom he came in contact, holding their respect and admiration by his simple kindness, which after all is the true measure of those really great, and

Whereas, his many years as a great hunter — ready in times of need, was never failing, one who was honored, respected and beloved.

Therefore, be it resolved that the Tulare Fish and Game

association extend to J. Bruce, the beloved master of our faithful friend, our deepest sympathy in his hour of sorrow, and

Be it further resolved, that these resolutions be entered in our minutes, one copy be sent to his master and one copy be entered in the official paper.

Walter C. Rice, President.

Geo. S. Lewis, Vice-President.

Jack Rogers, Secretary.

One evening in August 1938, Tommy Stephenson brought a dog to my camp, saying: "Here is a Basque shepherd I got from a sheepherder. I tried him out on bobcats at the ranch, and he trailed and treed two already, stayed at the tree and barked fast and furiously. I believe he will make a fine successor to Spike and last you as long as you'll want to keep on hunting lions, for he's only two years old. His name is Bosco. Judging by his appearance alone, I wouldn't have given two cents for all of his 25 pounds of heavy-coated, bushy-tailed, spindle-shanked body. But Tommy had said he trailed and treed two bobcats and that was all the recommendation I needed to give him a trial.

A couple of days later Bosco tasted lion blood for the first time and went cougar wild. A few more experiences and I had a worthy successor to Spike, who was showing signs of heart failure after seven years of strenuous effort on the cougar trails. Tommy had come through again in time of need, for Spike treed his last cougar one month later — in September, 1938 — after treeing eight during one week. It must have been grit alone that kept him going until the last cat was treed. For after the job was finished he collapsed and had to be carried a half-mile to our pickup truck, where he lay limp until we reached camp. Making a bed of pine needles I lifted his dying body and placed it gently on the bed. A few minutes later he uttered a groan of agony and his body went rigid — another faithful pal of mine had come to the end of the trail.

Diana had been retired the fall before, 1937, at the ripe old age of thirteen years. With her and Spike out of the running Bosco would have to take their place as a silent trailer and fast finisher.

In 1941 Bosco lost his life while hunting lions in Monterey County. Thereafter, until I retired in 1947, my principal hounds were Ranger IV and his little sister Diana II.

The events recorded herein are only a few out of several hundred which could be told about the dangerous and exciting adventures I shared with the faithful canine martyrs of the cougar hunts, Eli; Ranger I, II, III, IV; Scout, Bruce, Pete, Spike, Bud, Bosco, and Diana I, II, without whose constant devotion I never could have achieved the unequaled record of six hundred and sixty-nine cougars taken in the interest of preserving and increasing deer and domestic livestock throughout the "Golden State" of California.

V

TWO MEMORABLE COUGAR HUNTS

∧∧∧∧∧∧∧∧∧∧∧∧∧∧∧∧∧∧∧∧∧∧∧∧∧∧

Cougars Kill Porcupines with Impunity

HOW DO COUGARS manage to kill and eat prickly porcupines without collecting a mouthful or paw-full of porky's protective quills?

Lion hunters and naturalists, alike, have marveled at the big cat's ability to do this. But none of them have come up with the right answer so far. I spent some sixteen years on the lion trails before learning the methods practiced so cleverly by the felines to accomplish such a dangerous job of killing to obtain food in a pinch. During those years, I had found remains of many porcupines — perhaps a hundred — killed by the big cats, and went on to bag the killers, only to find them free of quills, or almost so — some having only a quill or two imbedded in paws or lips. In some cases the lions were jumped from bedding places close to their kills, leaving no doubt that they were the porcupine killers. Others were taken after I had trailed them several miles before bagging them, and then found porcupine flesh, including paws and claws, in their stomachs. There seems to be a reason for the presence of paws in the cougar diet, as we shall soon see.

First let me say that only members of the cat family can get away with the job of butchering and dressing any porcupine after the latter has developed its full growth of protective quills. I have seen dogs try it time and time again, only to give it up with a mouth, face and nose full of quills after a couple of bites at the seemingly easy prey. After every such

mistake it takes the combined strength and effort of two men
with a pair of pliers to relieve the dog of most of the misery
and restore its features to the semblance of what nature made
him, instead of the business end of a bristly paint brush. I
know because I have performed the operation on young, in-
experienced dogs many times.

Until an August day in my seventeenth year of lion hunting, every porcupine I had found partially devoured on the
lion trails had been killed on ground covered with leaves
and twigs shed by trees. Under such conditions no record of
the operation could be impressed in the ground. However,
I kept trying to picture in my mind a possible outline of the
procedure by which any member of the feline family could
accomplish the killing and eating of porcupines and at the
same time avoid being speared by the porcupine armor.

I got my first inkling of this procedure by recalling the
methods practiced by our house-cat to hook gophers that
were hiding in their burrows out of reach of the cat's mouth.
The cat takes a tactical position a foot or so from the opening
and out of line with the burrow. Situated thus, the cat keeps
out of sight of its prospective prey until the latter sticks its
head out to look around, or pushes out a load of dirt. Then
the cat springs. The gopher pulls in its head beyond reach
of the cat's teeth. It looks like pussy has been out-generaled.
But wait and see. Actually the rodent, following gopher procedure, has backed down no more than six inches before
turning a somersault to head farther down. During the instant it takes the gopher to change ends, the cat-paw makes a
swift pass underground, grips the rodent's back with five
unsheathed claws, gives a twisting yank, brings out the
doubled-up rodent and tosses it several feet from its refuge.
Surprised, torn and bleeding, the gopher tries to put up a
fight while its captor torments it by cuffing it around with
pricking claws. After a few minutes of this cat-play the
gopher refuses to play that way. To restore the rodent's interest in the gruesome game, pussy pretends to be looking
the other way. Seeing its chance, the gopher makes a run for

its burrow only to be hooked again and tossed farther away from its doorway. Finally the victim gets discouraged, gives up and sulks. Sensing the fun is over, the torturer presses a restraining paw on the victim's back and holds it down while ending the affair with a skull-crushing bite.

Here you see that the cat's paw was used to capture prey when it was not possible to do so with its mouth.

Now let's see how the big cats of the mountains operate with their paws to get by the porcupine armor and penetrate porky's defenses, while keeping their own nose, face and eyes out of contact with the hedge-hog's harmful quills.

I learned about this on an August morning in 1936, while trailing a male lion in the vicinity of Long Canyon in Placer County California. I was accompanied by a friend and companion of many lion hunts, Tommy Stephenson. Tommy was driving the state car at a speed of some 8 to 10 miles per hour, while I sat on the right front fender watching for lion tracks. Shortly after crossing the North Fork of Long Canyon Tommy slowed down and asked: "What kind of tracks are those ahead?" "Just a big porcupine's," I answered. Porky had walked in the dusty wheel tracks, just as all soft-footed animals do on roads to save wear on their sole-pads. A few hundred feet farther on Tommy stopped the car suddenly, just as I shouted: "whoa!" Four-inch cat tracks appeared in the dusty wheel-tracks across from porky's. Checking on the cat tracks, we noticed that their maker had come down a ten-foot bank from the uphill side of the road.

Tracks of both the porcupine and lion looked as though they had been made at about the same time during the night. If the porcupine had preceded the lion, there was a good chance that the predator would overtake the prospective prey before the latter left the road, get his supper and then bed in some thicket close by. Some two hundred feet farther on our prospective quarry had crossed over to porky's side of the road — just what we were hoping he had done, so we could learn which one was in the lead. Now we were thrilled to see the cat tracks had been impressed over those of the porcupine.

Probably the lion had noticed Porky's plain tracks and stalked the slow-poke, just as we were now hopefully stalking the potential killer, himself. As we drove along, tense with expectancy, the dogs in the screen-sided body behind us sensed our excitement, perked up and began whining while pressing their noses against the bars. Perhaps they already scented a kill ahead. We got a further thrill ourselves when we rounded the next turn, for tracks showed that the lion had suddenly lengthened his stride from 24 inches — normal walking steps, to a trotting length of 36 inches — evidence that he had sighted some possible prey ahead.

"Stop here and let's walk ahead and see what the lion was up to," I said.

Within the space of a hundred feet we found out. For tracks revealed that the trotting lion had overtaken the waddling porcupine. The latter, resorting to his usual method of defense, tucked his vulnerable head under his chest, thus presenting only the quill covered part of its anatomy to the potential killer. A circle of cat tracks showed how the latter had walked around the potential prey trying to locate its dangerous end. Meanwhile porky had given his enemy a clue, instead of the bluff intended, by slapping the ground with a heavily armed tail. Having learned which was porky's head end, the big feline sat down, cat fashion, and cautiously shoved a soft-toed forepaw under porky's nose and chin. This seemed like a harmless action, so porky, not wanting to start any trouble with the big cat, took it quietly. Meanwhile the insidious feline spread his caressing toes apart, feeling for porky's jugular vein and windpipe. At this stage, porky became suspicious of the cat's intentions and began maneuvering his tail-end slowly around to get in a position to slap the cat-paw. But the latter beat the porky tail to the blow by unsheating five wicked claws, pressing them against the porky throat, squeezing violently and puncturing the porcupine life lines, including the windpipe.

Whereupon porky tried to turn a somersault to bring his slapping tail into play, but the clever cat flipped his victim into the air, letting go his claw hold at the same instant. Porky landed six feet away, shedding scores of quills when hitting the ground. Fatally wounded, the porcupine ambled across the road and dragged itself toward a pine thicket, leaving a trail of blood along the way. The victorious cougar followed confidently until his bleeding victim passed out within fifty feet of the scene of attack. Now it was time for the feline meal. But how could the killer go about getting at the meat with his mouth and still prevent the quilled carcass from flopping against his face and eyes while tearing at it with his mouth?

Here is how it appeared to have been done: Hooking a claw into the porcupine chin or lip, the lion turned the body belly-upward and dragged it out from the jungle, where a blood-soaked spot of ground proved it had died of hemorrhage. Then, placing one cautious forepaw on the victim's bare throat and the other one on its pelvis, the big cat was ready to begin eating. But the porcupine chest and belly is flattish, thus presenting an object difficult to grip with the cat mouth, especially since the porky hide is tough. However, there are four other points to the porky anatomy free of quills and easy to grip with the feline mouth — the four paws sticking up right in the killer's face. The cat began by gnawing off a paw, and worked down the leg to the body line, swallowing every mouthful as he went. Now I knew why porcupine paws are so often found in stomachs of mountain lions.

This one devoured both forelegs of the victim, thus making an opening to the porcupine chest and belly. Then he was able to do a safe and clean job of eating porky out of its quilled hide. In this case the lion got his fill — some five or six pounds of meat — from the forelegs and trunk, leaving the hind legs and feet still attached to the hide.

After taking time out to read the details set down in the dust by the paws of the principals, we were ready to go after the clever killer. Several hours later, the dogs treed him. The lion was a sulky looking beast as he stood on a yellow-pine limb sixty feet up, with heaving sides, panting mouth and flattened ears.

Our only weapons consisted of a 22-caliber automatic pistol apiece, loaded with long-rifle cartridges. Any such weapon might be considered a feeble one with which to bring down a heavily muscled killer, armed with destructive teeth and claws and weighing 150 pounds — an animal capable of killing a full-grown steer, a man or several dogs within a few minutes. The use of such a weapon in cougar hunting might even seem ridiculous to anyone who had seen dozens of cougars spring from positions sixty to seventy five feet up in trees, when struck in the chest by bullets from large caliber, high-power rifles. Then after falling onto hard ground or rocks, get up and maul several dogs or run for several hundred feet and climb another tree. I have also seen many lions do the same things after being shot through their bodies several times by bullets from large caliber revolvers. Still, my favorite lion gun is the 22-caliber pistol. I prefer the pistol or revolver because the short gun is light and can be carried in a holster, leaving one's hands free to use in warding off limbs and twigs which threaten a hunter's eyes and face.

Let us see what happens when the same breed of cat absorbs the light, low-velocity bullets of a 22-caliber pistol. Tommy wanted to take the first shot at this one and aimed at a spot close back of the cat's shoulder-line. As the gun spat, the lion flinched. "Give him another one," I shouted. Tommy fired again. The cat stepped over to another limb. Then I tried a shot. The big cat flinched, hissed and looked around, seeking some cover. We were about to take aim again, when I noticed our target begin to sway and sag. "Don't shoot again. He's dying," I shouted. The next instant the big cat staggered off his perch and came crashing down, surrounded by broken limbs and twigs. The watching dogs, expecting a battle, separated to surround their quarry as it struck the ground, and then closed in to maul the quivering body.

While skinning our victim we found one porcupine quill imbedded in the cat's jaw and another one stuck in one ankle.

Further examination revealed that the little bullets from the squirrel guns had penetrated both lungs and caused hemorrhages which filled the chest cavity with blood. Thus, this cougar, member of a high-strung breed, had absorbed three fatal bullets without being knocked off his arboreal perch, or even being startled enough to send him leaping without looking. But this was only one instance, you might say. Well I have killed some 200 mountain lions and a dozen bears with this same gun and never had a dog injured by any animal shot with it. In nearly every case the dangerous predators died of hemorrhage while still out of reach of man and dogs. In most cases one little bullet did the job. So much for the 22-caliber pistol as a killer of big game at close range.

A Feline Amputee Makes Good in Surgery

Mankind has always been credited with being the most intelligent of all species of animal life. This may be so. But my experience with the so-called lower animals convinces me that they are endowed at birth with certain knowledge which human beings can acquire only at the expense of 20 years or more of study and work. For instance, every kind of fowl and four-footed animal can swim as soon as it can move its legs. Human beings have to be taught. Fowls and animals walk without aid from the first. Human beings have to learn the hard way.

So far we have considered a couple of physical attributes. Now let us consider skills on which one's life depends. If you were going about some necessary business in the woods and someone shattered your knee joint with a high powered 30-30 bullet and no doctor or surgeon could be had, would you trust a wild animal to amputate your leg and treat your wounds afterwards? Then suppose further that you had to get out, minus one limb, and rustle your own food while you were recuperating. Could you make good? Well, let's see how a wild animal handled a like misfortune without the benefit of medical or surgical training.

In June of 1939, I was hunting in the area adjoining the General Grand Grove of Big Trees. My companion was Ray Hutchison's son, Ed. We spotted lion tracks and turned the dogs loose. Soon Bosco began barking "treed." It had been a short chase — less than half a mile — but there was a good reason for our quarry treeing so quickly: she was heavy with young. One bullet from my 22-caliber Woodsman cut the aorta close to her heart, causing death by hemorrhage before she dropped from the tree.

Our camera was in the truck and Ed wanted a snapshot of himself carrying the panther. I photographed the cat's tracks made in the tire tracks of other cars, which had passed there a couple of days previously.

Tying the lioness on one front fender we drove to Logger Point tavern. A crowd soon gathered around to look at the carcass. Some of the people started to tell of how panthers had followed them through the woods after dark on several occasions and had screamed around their camp — experiences which never happened to me during fifty years spent in lion country. Of course, this adult lioness six feet long, and about to become a mother, was only a kitten compared to the size of lions some had seen dead or alive, according to the fantastic measurements they gave.

When we were about ready to start for camp a car arrived with two men in it. After sizing up the lion, one of them said to me: "I wish I had known how to get word to you last September." Of course, I asked him why. He replied: "I was driving along the road beyond the old Wortman sawmill on this side of Redwood Mt. and came around a short turn and right onto a female lion with three kittens about half the size of wildcats. I took a shot at the old lion while she was trying to shoo the kittens off the road, and knocked her down. Before I could get in another shot the mother lion scrambled up the bank and into the brush with her left foreleg dragging. The kittens disappeared in the brush at the lower side of the road."

"Why didn't you follow up the crippled cat and shoot

her again," I asked, "and then hide close by until the kittens
came out to look for their mother?"

"I wasn't going to mess around with any wounded lion in
the dark, when I didn't have a spotlight," he blurted out.
Without thinking, he had given away the fact that he was
hunting from a car at night, and thus was guilty on two counts
of violating the game laws. But what interested me was the
possibility that the lioness had been fatally wounded and that
the kittens might have been able to make a living by killing
fawns and rodents.

"We'll go over there tomorrow and see if we can find any
trace of those kittens," I told Ed.

After skinning the pregnant lioness I opened her up and
found that she would have become a mother of three kittens
within two weeks, every one female and so worth 30 dollars
each in bounty, had they been even one day old. I consoled
myself with the thought that a large number of deer had been
saved by preventing their birth.

The next day we drove over to Redwood Mountain and
checked carefully along the road described by the night-
hunter. Sure enough, lion tracks were there in the road a half
mile beyond the spot where the feline family had been seen
nine months before. But they were several days old and
dimly imprinted. I was able to make out tracks of four different sizes. Two sets appeared to have been made by kittens
about four months old — a male and a female. But there was
something confusing about the larger tracks. For instance,
some seemed to have been made by the rear paws of an average-sized adult female, with no front paw tracks to match,
while the only tracks made by an adult-sized front paw fitted
the paw of a yearling male.

The lions had come from the south and turned up mountain. I was unable to trace them on their forward course because the ground was covered by leaves or rocks. The day
after finding these signs, I was called away to make a hunt
for lions where tracks had been reported in the vicinity of
Camp Nelson in Tulare County.

On my way back to Millwood a month later, I met Art Bullard at Logger Point Tavern. He told me that he was just going to call me and report tracks of a female lion and two kittens. Arriving at Millwood late in the afternoon, I made camp, and then walked to the place where Art had seen the lion tracks, only a short hike from camp. There they were, just as I expected—the same sort of confusing lay-out of cat tracks I had found on Redwood Mountain, ten miles to the south, a month before.

Going back to the tracks next morning I traced them by sight for a mile or so toward the southeast and found the half-devoured carcass of a mother deer, with fresh-looking lion tracks all around it. The dogs got busy and trailed for several hundred feet up a gulch. There we found the hide of a spotted fawn with head and legbone attached. Trailing from here for a quarter-mile over a course half circular in shape, amongst brush and trees, we came around to a lay-out of rocks ideal for a panther hangout, and situated no more than a hundred yards south of the doe carcass. This panther-retreat consisted of three granite rocks some forty feet high, steep-walled and nearly flat on top. Two of them were separated from each other by a narrow crevice about one foot wide halfway down and narrowing until they pinched together at the ground level. The third one was as long as the other two put together and was separated from them by a passageway six to eight feet wide. Standing in this passageway, near its southwestern end was a large live oak tree, heavily branched and foliaged from its top down to the rocks on which some of the tree limbs rested.

I scanned the tree branches while the dogs traced the cat scent to the tree's base, sniffed the trunk as far up as they could reach and began barking "treed." The lions had climbed that tree, but were not hiding anywhere among its branches, so far as I could see. What had become of them? Maybe they had come down and prowled away in some other direction. I called the dogs and circled to find out.

Starting around the northern side I found a set of tracks

pointed away from the rock-bound arboreal panther-rest. This seemingly explained the lack of panthers in the tree, but it soon led to another confusing situation. The tracks showed that the whole panther group had prowled toward their hangout from this side, as well as having left it by this way. Analyzing the situation, I became convinced that the mysterious feline family was hiding in some invisible covert among the rocks.

Here is the way the evidence sized up: After killing the doe, and allowing the young cats to gorge themselves, the mother lion led them to the nearest suitable bedding place, one which, after she had explored it, appealed to her feline fancy as being just what Mother Nature had ordered for one in her condition, not to mention the family she had to care for. (What that condition was, we will learn in due time.)

After napping away the hours of daybreak in quiet seclusion, she led her youngsters back to the food cache under cover of darkness. As the trio of killers approached the scene, a motherless fawn bounded away from its point of vigil close to the mutilated corpse of its mother. The sharp cat-eyes followed the fleeing fawn until it disappeared in a thicket. Now the mother cat had work to do while her youngsters were enjoying a feast all ready prepared for them. Leading them to the doe carcass, she dragged it out from under the pile of leaves which she had raked over it to keep in the tell-tale odor and keep out polluting flies during the daytime. Then giving her offsprings the feline sign to stay put, she pussy-footed to the exact spot where the infant deer had reached cover. The panther nose and eyes together soon located the cringing fawn. A swift rush and Mrs. Felis had a death grip on it. After dining on the tender meat and drinking from a spring nearby, she returned to her gorged youngsters, leading them up the gulch to water. From there the family took a walk, following the round-about course over which the dogs trailed them to their bedding place, and were now secreted there.

The young lions might be hiding in the crevice, but their

mother would be more likely to crouch on top of one of the three rocks. The only way I could spot them was to climb up some tree tall enough for the purpose. After sizing up every tree standing within pistol range of the lion refuge I found that all of them — mostly large black-oaks — were bereft of limbs as far up as twenty feet above the ground. Then I got another idea: Maybe I could get a view of the rock tops from some place on the hillside to the north or east. I tried that, but found my view obstructed by wide-spreading, heavily foliaged black-oaks or bushy cedar and pine saplings growing all along a semicircular course on a level with the cougars' elevated refuge. Low ground lying to the south and extending around to the northwest prevented me from viewing the rock-tops from that direction. Whether our sagacious quarry had chosen this impregnable lair by accident or by design, we do not know. In any event, it provided them with total protection from the eyes and guns of mankind — the only enemy they feared to cope with in battle.

Therefore, I spent the balance of the morning examining every possibility of getting a shot at one of the cougars. I know, too, that if anyone of them was missing when they "counted noses" before leaving there, the others would hang around for several hours, trying to find the missing one, or return several times for such purpose, thus providing fresh tracks. Next, I thought of lying in wait in some covert within pistol range in hopes that one or another would become restless and show itself. After trying this plan for a couple of hours without success, I decided to go to camp — a half a mile away —have lunch and rest. If the lions tried to sneak away while I was gone the dogs would be able to pick up the new tracks. Sure enough, this is what happened. When I went back the next morning, the dogs picked fresh lion tracks north of the impregnable lair. The three cats were headed north. The hounds followed the scent toward a gulch leading to Abbott Creek.

A mile down the gulch, I heard a staccato barking in the distance that indicated the hounds had one lion treed. I hoped it was the big one. Loading my revolver I approached quietly. Yes, it was the she cat standing on limbs of a small tree and no more than fifteen feet up. I expected her to make a jump when she saw me, but she only shifted a bit and kept a pair of wild-looking eyes at us. I didn't notice then that one of her legs was missing below the elbow. But apparently she was aware of her handicap, for she failed to react to the impact of a bullet as most lions do, by leaping out regardless of where they would land. One bullet through the chest ended her remarkable career of supporting her family, while having only three legs to go on.

With their leader gone the young lions should have been quite easy to tree. But I had a good reason for not disposing of them at once, even though I might find them hiding in a tree. For one thing, I wanted to take them alive to fill an order from the Orient. But I had neglected to bring along ropes for that purpose.

I could come back tomorrow, equipped with ropes and sacks with which to capture them alive. But I would need some help to handle the two cats and the dogs, especially since we would have to carry the former for a mile to reach the nearest road. Two of the young fellows in town offered to help me with the capture and were excited about the prospects of taking a hand in the venture.

The two boys failed to show up on time the next morning. Nevertheless, I set out to try and handle the cougars alone. I had done it before, one at a time, and had my hands full. Taking only two dogs, Ranger and Bosco, I drove down to Abbott Creek, left the pickup and walked up the gulch I had followed while bringing the lioness out yesterday. Since the air currents were still moving down gulch, the cats couldn't get wind of us in time to give them a head-start toward some bluffs where they could hide in crevices or on ledges, inaccessible to man and dogs.

While trying to approach stealthily, my worst trouble was keeping the dogs under control and silent after they sniffed lion scent carried in the air current. To avoid this I bore off to the east several hundred feet and so managed to approach close enough to surprise the wary felines at their breakfast.

As the dogs rushed in, the cats took off in different directions, with Bosco taking after one and Ranger chasing the other. Bosco began barking "treed" within a few seconds and less than two hundred feet from the starting point, while Ranger was still chasing his quarry, baying at every jump. I went to Bosco and found him barking up at a twenty-five pound, snarling panther clinging to the topmost branches of a pine sapling twenty feet tall. Then came the sounds of claws tearing tree bark and the crackling of dry limbs some three hundred feet down gulch, followed by Ranger telling me his cat was treed. Those sounds indicated that Ranger's quarry had taken to a good-sized tree, having only small dry limbs up to twenty feet or more above the ground, and would stay there as long as dogs were barking anywhere nearby.

I needed a pole six feet long, and got one by cutting down a slender fir sapling, trimmed off all the limbs except one close to the tip, which I left four inches long. Then I formed a slip-noose on one end of a fifty-foot length of quarter-inch rope, tied it around my waist, took the pole and climbed the tree to within six feet of the uneasy young panther, who seemed to be trying to make up her mind whether to risk battling the dog or man. I helped her decide by staying six feet below her, so that by the time I had freed the rope from my own body and hooked the loop over the pole-tip, young Miss Felis appeared to have gained some confidence in her ability to bluff me. She even refrained from any violent actions yet keeping suspicious eyes on every movement of the loop and pole as I pushed it up past her head. But when I tried to let the loop down around her nervous head, the cat's paw, with claws unsheated, warded it off with a vicious thrust, while her teeth tested the pole for signs of life.

After several repeat performances, which seemed to convince her that this contrivance was not a living thing, she finally began regarding the snare with more curiosity than resentment until the loop began setting down around her head. Then sensing a trap she snapped at the rope with her mouth and held on firmly.

Freeing the pole-tip from the loop, I maneuvered it around to the back of her head and worked that part of the loop down around her neck. This move brought on a fear of attack from behind and caused the lion to spit out the rope and twist her head around to bite at the pole again, an action which let the freed loop drop and encircle her neck. Giving a sudden jerk, I tightened it and had her roped temporarily.

But I couldn't go away and leave her this way for even a few minutes, for she could loosen the loop with a paw and push it off over her head and get away. Or she might jump out of the tree and hang herself over a limb, while I was trying to rope her brother. I would have to bring her to the ground and change the slip noose to one which could not be loosened, or tightened enough to choke her to death. First, I tied Bosco back out of reach — twenty-five feet from the cat's tree. Then I pulled at the rope, until the cat had to come down head-first, clawing at branches to keep from falling.

Landing on the ground she rushed toward a thicket, came to the end of her rope, and flopped over. She got up and began biting and clawing at the tightened loop around her neck. I pulled the rope tight enough partly to cut off her breathing, causing her to roll over. Then I grabbed her tail with one hand, stepped on her rope close to her neck and knelt down, pressing one knee on her hips and the other one on her shoulders. Held thus, our captive could move only her head, while I cut the rope some five yards from her neck and tied a knot that couldn't loosen or tighten. Getting my camera out of my knapsack I took a picture of our captive.

Bosco, who had been intently watching, now thought he should be allowed to go a round or two with the grounded panther, and began whimpering and tugging to be released. To avoid this I tried to herd the cougar up a tree so that she would be out of reach of the hounds' mouths. But catlike she refused to be guided. Instead she rolled over on her back and defied me by presenting four sharp-clawed paws — the favorite position taken by any feline on the defensive. That neither coaxing nor bluffing would change her attitude, I knew from experience. I would have to take her in hand and boost her far enough up a tree to make her think she was getting away, then she would do her part.

Dragging her to a forked oak I grabbed hold of her tail with one hand and gripped the loop back of her neck with my other hand and started to lift her off the ground to toss her up into the tree crotch. Then the agile feline went into real action. Snarling, spitting, twisting and waving all four paws, she got a claw-hold on my legs and started to climb me instead of the tree. Before I could shout scat panther, she made a bloody trail of claw-marks up to my shoulders and clung there with eight fore-paw-claws hooked through my denim jumper and into my chest muscles, while as many hind-paw-claws raked my abdomen, Next, the sharp-toothed cat's mouth opened wide before my face blowing blast after blast of tainted feline spittle against my face, while wild cat-eyes glared into my eyes. Here was only twenty-five pounds of feline fury pitted against eight times her weight of manpower. But she had the advantage of being armed with natural weapons, and in a position to use them against the most vulnerable part of my anatomy, my eyes, bare face, and neck. The panther's teeth and claws could puncture my windpipe or jugular vein if she took a notion to attack that way, or, if she clawed my good right eye, I would be totally blinded.

My situation was somewhat like that of a porcupine when it feels the claws of a cougar searching for its throat, in that I dared not make any movement which might provoke the cat to attack first. I never will know just what influenced this one to hesitate for those awful seconds while we eyed each other across a space of less than one foot. Maybe she too feared to make the next move. As it turned out neither one of us, man or cat, had to make the final decision, for Ranger, hearing the feline snarls, came running up to take part in whatever was going on, letting out a lusty roar on sighting the panther within his reach. At the same time, Bosco, fearing he

would miss something, went wild with voice and action trying to get free to join the fracas. Ranger, baying furiously,
raced toward us. The menacing panther let go in a hurry
and sprang backward away from me, just in time to dodge
the hound's grasp at her, and the next instant began climbing
hastily up the very tree I had chosen to park her in. Seeing
that she would soon take her rope leash up beyond my reach,
I rushed to get hold of the lower end and fasten it to a limb
some six feet up.

Now it looked like our feline captive would be safe while I
gave all my attention to capturing her brother. I released
Bosco, called both dogs, and went down gulch looking for the
tree which Ranger had been barking up before he came to
help me.

I would have to depend on the hound to lead me to it.
When we reached the tree to which Ranger had chased the
cat, the young panther was gone, evidently losing little time
in getting away. The dogs picked up the trail and raced along
baying furiously.

The dogs were headed toward Abbott Creek and my truck,
which would be just fine if young "Tommy" happened to
take refuge in a small tree this time. He had already saved me
the task of lugging him a half mile, when Bosco began barking as though he had the cat bayed on the ground. A few seconds later Ranger caught up to the fighting Bosco. I raced
frantically through underbrush and over fallen trees trying
to reach the scene of battle in time to save the cat from being
mauled to death.

Meanwhile, the feline snarls and yowls were becoming
spasmodic and feeble, ceasing altogether by the time I got
there. Then, I saw at a glance that it was all over but the
skinning. This I did on the spot and hung the hide on a tree
to be picked up later on. Now, with one cat out of the way,
bringing the other one in alive should be an easy task.
Unfortunately, when I got back to her, I found she had tried
her brother's stunt, trying to get away, but ended up hanging
herself.

Again I consoled myself with the knowledge that the elimination of this feline family would save more than a thousand deer from suffering a gruesome death by their teeth and claws.

Now I turned to the fascinating problem of figuring out how the three-legged mother had managed to survive the initial wound and eventually recover to the point where she could sustain herself and two kittens. How had she managed to amputate one leg and survive without the benefit of veterinary surgery, hospitalization and provision for proper food? Certainly, she was not able to hunt deer when suffering acute pain, weakened from loss of blood and disabled with a foreleg shattered so seriously that it had to be amputated at the elbow. Even after the amputation had been accomplished she would have been required to lie low for a couple of weeks, at least, before attempting to hunt and kill any other animal in order to secure necessary food. Then how did she secure that needed food?

To begin with we have evidence to show that this three-legged lioness was the one crippled by the night-hunter's shot eleven months before we caught her. For instance, you will remember that he told me that he got in one shot which knocked the lioness over. She got up and scrambled up the bank and out of sight among some bushes, dragging her left foreleg — the same one missing from the body of this she-cougar. Then, too, I had first found her tracks on the very road being traveled by the lioness seen by the night-hunter, and close to the scene of the shooting that night (cougars habitually travel the same beat year after year) .

Those over-sized front paw tracks which I first found there identified this three-legged female panther as having been the one who made them. The unusually large front paw print for a female was explained by the fact that one over-worked foreleg and paw had been developed to nearly twice its normal size by doing double duty for nearly a year, while she carried on a normal cougar life of breeding, bearing and rearing a normal litter of offspring.

Now, after having connected the cougar disability with the night-hunter's bullet, let us go on and explain how she managed to secure food while suffering from the shock and pain induced by such a serious wound and weakened from loss of blood.

First, we can assume that she had killed a deer while hunting alone several hours before she was wounded. Why are we so sure of this? Well, we know from long experience that the mother cougar never allows her kittens to accompany her on a hunt until they become old enough to know what it is all about — say six months of age. This one's kittens, at the time of the shooting, were probably about two months old, and would not have been traveling with their dam unless she was leading them to a fresh kill. (I am judging their age by the description of their size as given by the night hunter.)

Now, suppose that her kill was only a half-mile from the scene of the shooting, or even a mile, she could still manage to lead her kittens to it. Then by rationing it out to her young she could make it last to feed all of them for a week, provided it was a full-grown deer. If it was a doe, she or the kittens could lay in wait for the motherless fawn and secure food for another day or two. But what did the crippled cat do after her natural food supply became exhausted? There is only one thing she could do to survive, something the law of self-preservation would dictate — making use of the only available food, she turned cannibalistic and devoured her own offspring, one at a time. The kittens should have weighed eight pounds, at least, and should have provided sustenance for the adult lion for five days. Thus, her three kittens would sustain her for fifteen days. Adding seven days rations of venison, and allowing that she or her kittens devoured her own forearm after she had amputated it with her teeth, and we can understand how this crippled, wild creature managed to survive until her wound had healed. As for water, that could be found in numerous springs and rivulets common to this area.

After three weeks of self care, the crippled cougar should

have been able to get around well enough to make a living by preying on ground squirrels, tree squirrels, fawns and even calves younger than four months of age. As her strength returned and she became used to operating on three legs she would naturally develop a method of approaching, attacking and holding her prey which could overcome any full-grown doe, yearling buck or weaned calf.

What reason have we to assume that this feline mother sacrificed her offspring to serve her own needs? Well, they should have been able to make a living for themselves after their dam became disabled. (I have known lion kittens eight weeks old to do so by preying on rodents and fawns and following their sire or some other adult feline killer — at a safe distance — and sitting at second table for several meals at each opportunity.)

Furthermore, if kittens had survived they would have been nearly a year old and still traveling together when we trailed their mother to her death. Yet we found no sign of yearling lions anywhere along the beat used regularly by the crippled cat, and the same beat over which she had led her last year's litter, when, surprised and blinded by headlights, she was shot by the night hunter.

Considering all the accomplishments of this resourceful wild animal, the one which impressed me as being the most remarkable was the neat job of surgery she had performed on her shattered limb.

The stump had healed cleanly and was covered smoothly by tough skin. I venture to say that no veterinary surgeon could have taught this feline any tricks.

*   *   *

Looking back over the years of my life, I cannot help but marvel at my good fortune. I think of my childhood days, beset by almost incredible hardships, yet happy withal because of the closeness to nature. I recall the thrills of forking rattlers for cash, hooking trout to order, hunting all kinds of wild game to put meat on the table. I compare the acquired and unnatural meanness of humans with the instinctive and natural ferocity of wild animals, and find myself preferring the latter. I realize now, after having gone through similar experiences, how much the pioneers suffered to make America the great nation it is today. I am grateful indeed for the many friendships I made — friendships that were all the warmer and truer because they were forged in common peril and labor.

I review the hundreds and hundreds of hunts — each different and yet all basically alike — unfolding an orderly pattern of life with each new experience, until a clear picture of wild life emerged in all its beauty and intricacy. I marvel that I survived the hazards with no more than a crippled hand, one lost eye and innumerable close calls. I find it difficult to believe that a human body could have spent over three score years and ten in the wilds, climbing up and down an incredible number of miles of rough terrain, often under the most adverse of conditions.

Yes, I marvel at my good fortune and fervently thank the fates for the opportunity to spend my life in the primeval forest among nature's wild creatures. I commiserate with those who, seeking to do the same, find that civilization is inexorably causing that opportunity to disappear.

www.ingramcontent.com/pod-product-compliance
Lightning Source LLC
Chambersburg PA
CBHW050221270326
41914CB00003BA/518